CONCISE DICTIONARY OF HOLIDAYS

Concise Dictionary
of Holidays

RAYMOND JAHN

PHILOSOPHICAL LIBRARY
New York

Manufactured in the United States of America

LIST OF ILLUSTRATIONS

PLATE

FOREWORD

Each of us has a private calendar to which we refer for private calculations. We reckon time by days which are special days for us, and so, in a larger sense, does mankind. Whenever a significant portion of any population anywhere chooses to remember a pleasure, an act of kindness, a death, that special day is set aside. By these calculations we keep track of our history, our principles, our very humanity. Whether important for their secular or spiritual significance, these days are important for fun, for thanksgiving, but most of all for remembering.

This is a dictionary of days we have set apart—of holidays, holy days, special days, festivals, feasts, fasts, birthdays and anniversaries. But it is not intended as a complete dictionary of all days everywhere; it is meant primarily to include days which might come to an American's attention, provided he is the sort of American who is interested in all sorts of fellow Americans. Neither is it designed merely as a reference work, a stuffy compendium for the library shelf; the reader will find hints here of the wonderful diversity (and essential sameness) of people who meet in America and whom Americans meet.

This short dictionary includes principal holidays of all major faiths, state days of all states, anniversaries of most nations, and many occasions remembered from days before we celebrated new and American holidays. For the information in this book the editor is indebted to ambassadors and persons in government and state employ all over the world, and to men of many faiths.

All have generously provided information and given counsel. In addition I would like especially to thank the publishers of the following books for information which formed a basis for comparison whenever discrepancies appeared: The American Library Association (Mary Hazeltine, ANNIVERSARIES AND HOLIDAYS, 1944), Ernest Benn (Eleanor Graham, HIGH DAYS AND HOLIDAYS, 1932), Harcourt, Brace (Francis Weiser, THE HOLYDAY BOOK, 1956), Little, Brown and Co. (Joseph Gaer, HOLIDAYS AROUND THE WORLD, 1953), Wm. Sloane Associates (Theodor Gaster, FESTIVALS OF THE JEWISH YEAR, 1953), and The Woman's Press (Dorothy Gladys Spicer, THE BOOK OF FESTIVALS, 1937).

R. Jahn

CONCISE DICTIONARY OF HOLIDAYS

Ab: The Fast of Ab, *(Tisha b'Ab)* a Jewish fast day, falls on the 9th day of Ab, the fifth sacred month of the Jewish calendar; therefore it is known as The Fast of the Fifth Month (Zech. 8:19 and Jer. 52:12). It is possible that this celebration is related to the "Festival of the Firewood" celebrated by the Babylonians during the month of Ab. The 9th of Ab is a day of mourning historically associated with the destruction of the Temple in 586 B.C.E. and in 70 C.E. See *Destruction of the Temple.*

Adar: A minor Jewish fast day *(Tannit Esther)* on the thirteenth of Adar, is celebrated in memory of Queen Esther and the fast she proclaimed when informed of the decree of Ahasuerus ordering the destruction of her people.

Abraham's Sacrifice: Mohammedan holiday commemorating Abraham's sacrifice to the Lord, celebrated the tenth day of the Moslem month. See *'Id al-Adha.*

Adam and Eve: The day before Christmas was popularly known as "Adam and Eve Day" in Hungary. Special services were held and traditional food prepared.

Adam's Birthday: The weekly day of rest in Islam, called Yaum al-Jum'ah (which see). The faithful of Islam believe that Adam was born on Friday and on a Friday was taken into Paradise.

Admission: In some state the date of admission into the federation of United States is celebrated as a legal and bank holiday. The custom and name given the occasion, however, differ with the various states and territories. Two states, Arizona and California, refer to this anniversary as "Admission Day"; Idaho and Utah employ the name "Pioneer Day."

Advent: Advent is not, properly speaking, a holiday; it is the liturgical season which begins the Church year in preparation for the celebration of Christmas. Advent begins on the Sunday nearest St. Andrew's Day, November 30th, and lasts the four weeks preceding Christmas. This period, one of the three major divisions of the ecclesiastical year, is variously marked by solemn observances, sometimes with traditional folk and local customs as well, all of a penitential character.

St. Agatha: St. Agatha, virgin, martyred in 251 in Sicily, was said miraculously to have freed her people from Etna's eruption and to have kept them from starvation. Veneration of St. Agatha as patroness against starvation and fire spread to the Continent and became especially popular in Switzerland. The Agatha bell, rung at the beginning of the year, invoked her intercession in Switzerland. In Sicily "Agatha loaves" were blessed as protection against fires.

St. Agnes: Patron saint of young girls, martyred in the time of Diocletian for refusing the love of Olybius, a Roman Prefect of Antioch. St. Agnes Day was, especially in England, a favorite day for weather prognostication, where it was thought possible for a girl on St. Agnes Eve to see in her dreams the man she later would marry. The Feast of St. Agnes was held to be a special holiday; in England female labor was forbidden on this day, the 21st of January.

Alaska: The formal transfer of the Territory of Alaska from Russia to the United States was made on October 18, 1867, at Sitka. October 18th is observed as a holiday; Alaska Day, in the Territory.

Allahabad: The Hindu Makara Sankranti or New Year celebration of the winter season is an occasion for purification and bathing in the River Ganges. Many devout Hindus make a pilgrimage to Allahabad, the City of God, at this season, is also known as the Month of the Holy Fair at Allahabad.

Almo: Alamo Day is celebrated in Texas on the 6th of March in commemoration of the victory over Mexico at the seige of the Almo at San Antonio, which began February 23, 1836.

All Fools: See *April Fools' Day.*

All Hallomas (Allhallows): See *All Saints' Day.*

All Saints: Instituted by Pope Boniface IV to celebrate the changing of the Pantheon ("all demons") at Rome into a Christian Church, in memory of the Virgin Mary and All Martyrs. During the reign of Gregory IV the date was changed to November 1st. The occasion is now interpreted as an occasion for honoring all dead saints, particularly those who might not otherwise receive special homage. Celebrated by the Greek Orthodox Church on or about July 1st. Louisiana observes All Saints' Day, November 1st, as a legal holiday.

All Souls: The 2nd of November is set aside by the Roman Catholic Church on behalf of souls in Purgatory. Priests may on this day say three masses. Observance of All Souls Day is said to have arisen at the monastery of Cluny in the ninth century. The day has come to have a more general significance in many quarters as a time set aside for prayers for all the dead, and as such as been insttiuted in certain Protestant churches.

St. Ambrose: The Feast of St. Ambrose is celebrated in the Roman Church in honor of one of the great Latin Fathers of the Church. Ambrose was made Bishop of Milan in 374; in 381 he was declared president of a synod of bishops at Aquileia.

American Indian: Several states of this country set aside a special day in honor of Indians living within their borders. New York, the first state to establish this custom, observes American Indian Day on the fourth Friday in September. Publicity was first given the American Indian when, in 1913, Red Fox James, of the Blackfeet Nation, rode several thousand miles on a pony to urge states to adopt such celebrations.

Anden Paaskedag: Among the Danes Easter Monday is a great holiday. It is called "Second Easter." See *Easter*.

St. Andrew: The feast day of St. Andrew, follower of John the Baptist and first of the twelve apostles, called by Christ, is observed on November 30th. He is said to have suffered martyrdom (about 70 A.D.) on an X-shaped cross which is associated with his name and with this date. Relics of his body, which was thereafter interred, were, according to tradition, conveyed to Constantinople and thence to the coast of Fife. St. Andrew is Scotland's patron saint; Andrys' Day or Andermess is, throughout Scotland and parts of England, a popular occasion for sporting and local observances.

St. Anne: Festivals in honor of St. Anne, mother of the Blessed Virgin Mary, are celebrated throughout all Catholic countries. Perhaps the most famous of these is to be found at Auray, in Brittany. Each year many people make pilgrimage to *Le Pardon de Sainte Ann d'Auray* on her day, the 26th of July.

Anniversary: Australia Day was frequently known as Anniversary Day before 1930; in New South Wales, Australia Day still is known by this name.

Annunciation: In Roman Catholic and Greek Orthodox countries, a great festival, in the Anglican Church a feast, also noted in Protestant congregations. In England commonly called Lady Day, in France *Notre Dame de Mars.* Celebrated on March 25th, in commemoration of the Virgin Mary's presentiment of the birth of Christ. (Luke 1:26.)

St. Anthony: The Catholic Church recognizes the feast day of St. Anthony, confessor, on June 13th and of St. Anthony, "patriarch of all monks," on January 17th. St. Anthony, Franciscan confessor, was known as the "miracle worker" and "hammer of heretics." But the latter, who is generally regarded as the father of Christian monasticism, is one of the more familiar figures of Catholic hagiology. He it was who, during the Middle Ages, became popular as the patron saint of animals; numerous folk customs illustrate the point. In Spain the Dia de San Anton is occasion for blessing all four-footed farm beasts, and in Mexico San Antonio Abad is looked on as a time when all domestic animals should be suitably decorated and blessed by the priests. The excellent Chambers in his *Book of Days* gives a detailed exposition of mock trials of dumb animals held by English revelers in sport of the occasion.

St. Anthony of Padua is the patron saint of Portugal; his feast day falls on the 13th of January.

Anzac: Anzac Day derives its name from the first letters of the Australian and New Zealand Army Corps, and the day, the 25th of April, derives its signficance from the landing of Australian and New Zealand troops at Gallipoli, in World War I. Anzac Day is a national holiday in Australia in commemoration of this event.

Apple Tuesday: The New York Fruit Growers Association

voted in 1905 to urge the adoption of Apple Tuesday on the recommendation of the Louisiana Purchase Exhibition in St. Louis the preceding year. The movement has had some success in the intervening years.

Appomattox: Lee's surrender of the Army of Northern Virginia to General Grant at Appomattox in 1865 commemorates the restoration of the Union. The occasion has been celebrated by Civil War Veterans of Grand Army posts especially, and, at various times, by other organizations throughout the country.

April Fast: See *Fast Day*, a legal holiday in New Hampshire.

April Fools: A holiday of mind, not of state. The tradition of setting aside some special day for making a fool out of other people has its roots in antiquity, but the habit of playing jokes on people and making them run fool's errands is not confined to any nationality or time. It is probable that the custom became associated with April 1st when, in 1564, Charles IX of France adopted a calendar which made January 1st rather than April 1st the new year's first day. April fooling appears to have been customary in England by the eighteenth century. During the Middle Ages the "Feast of the Ass" was celebrated on Twelfth Day (after Christmas) with unclerical splendor, guilds and other secular organizations participating. The Feast of the Ass (which see) served a similar social function to our April 1st.

Arab League Pact: *'Id-al-Jami'a al-Arabiyyah.* In Jordan the anniversary of the Arab League Pact, signed March 22, 1945, is celebrated as a national holiday.

Arbor: In nearly every state, some parts of Canada, and some countries, a special day is set aside for planting trees and shrubs. In this Hemisphere the date is often March 7th, Luther Burbank's birthday, but the date may differ according to local traditions and climate, as may the manner of observance itself. Arbor Day was first proclaimed in Nebraska in 1872; on this occasion over a million trees were planted throughout the state. In 1922 President Harding urged governors of all states to set aside April 22nd in honor of J. Sterling Morton, who sponsored the first Arbor Day, but Burbank's birth date later took precedence.

Argentine: National Independence Day in Argentina is celebrated on July 9th. Argentine independence from Spanish rule was formally declared in 1816. This same occasion is celebrated in the city of Buenos Aires on the 25th of May.

Arjun: See *Sikh Holidays*.

Armistice: November 11th is a legal holiday in only twenty-one of the United States, though the date is annually observed by gubernatorial proclamation in others. This occasion is usually obesrved by a parade and fitting tribute to those who died in World War I, since November 11th marks the signing of the Armistice. In Canada it is called Remembrance Day.

By Act of Congress in 1945 Armistice Day was changed to Veterans' Day, so that it might include tribute to the country's defenders of the Second World War. It is known, at the present time, as Veterans' Day in most states, Victory Day in others. In Alabama and Florida the term "Armistice" Day is still preferred.

Army: Established by Presidential proclamation in 1927 to commemorate the United States's entrance into World War I.

Army Stitch: Armistice Day, U. S. Slang.

Ascension: An ecumenical feast day celebrating Christ's ascent into heaven, and one of the first festivals of the Christian Church, both in importance and in origin, since it was probably instituted by the apostles. Ascension Thursday is celebrated as a general holiday in most European countries. forty days after Easter. It is also called Holy Thursday (see *Quinto-Feirada Espiga*) and is preceded by the Rogation Days.

Ash Wednesday: The first day of Lent, the period of Christian penance in preparation for Easter. The day derives its name from the use of ceremonial ashes worn as a symbol of penitence. (Among reformed churches this practice has fallen into disuse.) Ash Wednesday is preceded by Shrove

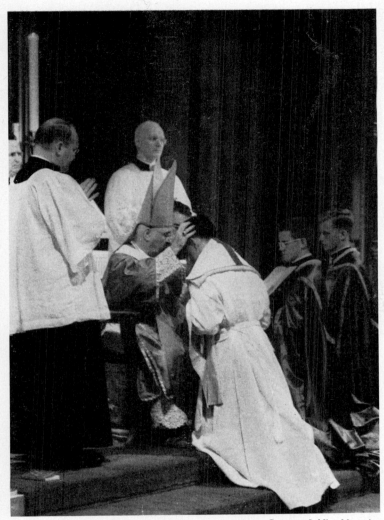

PLATE 1

The Ordination of a Priest

In the Roman Catholic Church, the Bishop (in this picture Cardinal Spellman), acting as successor of the Apostles, lays his hands on the head of George Moore and transmits to him the office of priesthood.

PLATE 2

Procession of the Penitents at Veurne, Belgium.

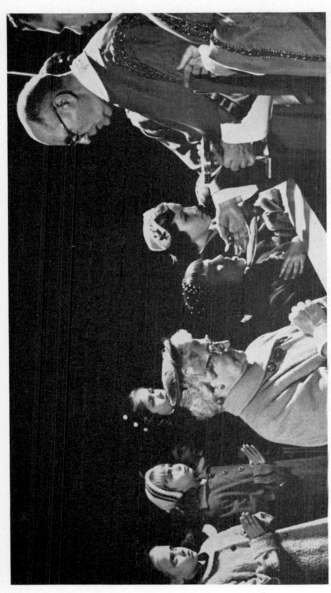

PLATE 3

The Eucharistic Banquet

Communicants receiving the Holy Eucharist, high point of the Roman Catholic Mass.

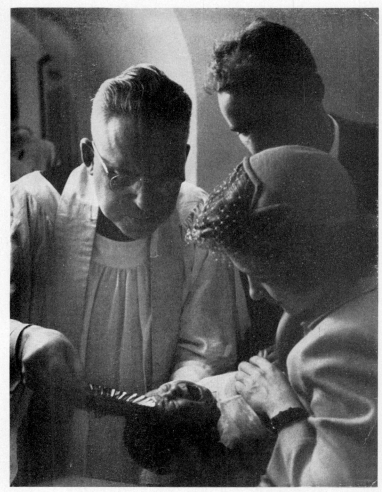

PLATE 4

Baptism

Pouring water in the form of a cross, the Catholic priest baptizes in the name of the Father, Son and Holy Ghost.

PLATE 5

During the Easter Vigil in the Catholic Church, the paschal candle
is plunged into the baptismal water.

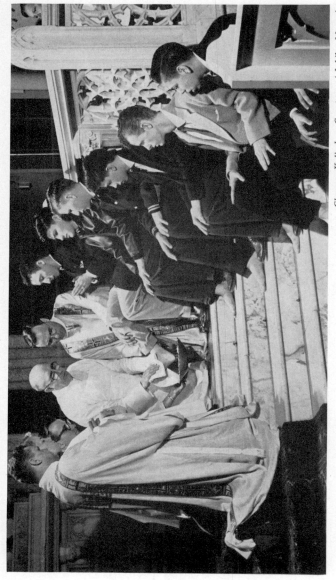

PLATE 6

After the Gospel of the Holy Thursday evening Mass in the Catholic Church, the pastor, following the example of Christ at the Last Supper, washes the feet of some of his parishioners. This ceremony keynotes Holy Thursday as a day of fraternal charity.

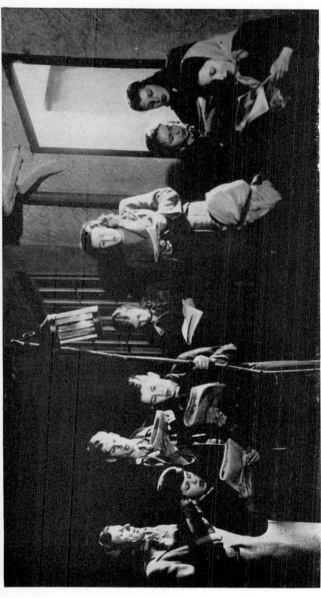

PLATE 7

English Carol Singers

For some nights before Christmas, singers go from house to house singing carols. Carols have been sung at this time of year for hundreds of years. A carol may perhaps be defined as a religious song, less formal and solemn than the usual church hymn. The most popular carols today date from the eighteenth century. The tradition of "waits," or small gatherings of people going from house to house, is so old its exact origin has been forgotten.

PLATE 8

Strange Customs of the City of London

The Vintners' Company procession, headed by sweepers, on its way to the Church of St. James in London, a ceremony which takes place each July 12. Two wine porters walk ahead, wearing clean aprons and carrying brooms, with which they go through the form of sweeping the streets, a relic of days when London's streets were filthy and evil-smelling. Members of the Company carry bundles of sweet-smelling flowers and herbs for a similar purpose.

אִישׁ
וְאֵת

פַּרְשַׁנְדָּתָא
וְאֵת

דַּלְפוֹן
וְאֵת

אַסְפָּתָא
וְאֵת

פּוֹרָתָא
וְאֵת

אֲדַלְיָא
וְאֵת

אֲרִידָתָא
וְאֵת

פַּרְמַשְׁתָּא
וְאֵת

אֲרִיסַי
וְאֵת

אֲרִדַי
וְאֵת

וַיְזָתָא
עֲשֶׂרֶת

From a Megillah of the 14th Century

PLATE 9

Purim Holiday of the Hebrews

The hanging of the sons of Haman, who had set the day for the
extermination of all Jews in Babylon. The plot was uncovered and
he was duly punished.

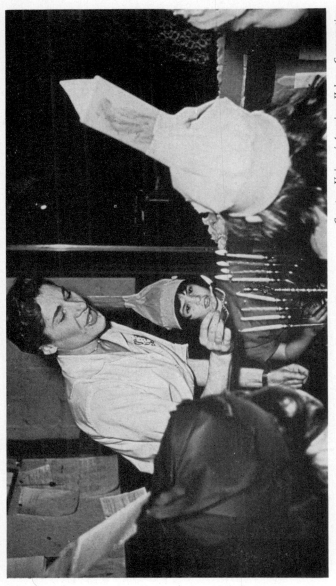

PLATE 10

Chanukah: Hebrew Festival of Lights

Lighting the Menorah in the classroom of a religious school.

PLATE 11

Rosh Ha-Shanah

Blowing the shofar during the services of the Hebrew holiday, Rosh Ha-Shanah.

PLATE 12
New Year's in Greece

The Prime Minister is cutting the traditional cake of St. Basil containing a lucky coin, a Greek New Year's custom.

PLATE 13

Easter in Greece

An evzone from the King's Guard cracks eggs with a friend, an ancient Easter custom in Greece.

From the Japanese work Miao Tsi T'u Lu

PLATE 14

Laotse.

宣聖遺像

唐吳道子作

From an 8th Century portrait by Wu Tao Tsi

PLATE 15

Confucius.

PLATE 16

Japanese Statue of Buddha.

Tuesday in the week beginning with Quinquagesima Sunday. In many countries Ash Wednesday is a strict day of fast.

Ashura: Mohammedan anniversary of Noah's sailing forth in the ark from Mount Ararat, celebrated about the 10th day of the first moon month, Muharram. *'Ashura* is the name of a sweet holiday food especially favored among Mohammedans in celebration of this day. For *Asarah be-Tebet,* see Tebet.

Ass: The Feast of the Ass which, according to one authority, was supposed to have been celebrated on Twelfth Day (see *April Fools' Day*), according to another on the 14th of January, originally commemorated the Flight of the Holy Family into Egypt. Theatrical representations of the trip taken by Mary, Joseph and the Christ Child lost, as traditional theatrical productions are apt to, almost all pious decorum. One of the popular figures in productions of the late Middle Ages was the ass of the manger; indeed, he became so popular that occasion for such ribald comedy came to be called the Feast of the Ass.

Assumption of the Virgin Mary: The miraculous ascent into heaven of the Blessed Virgin Mary is celebrated through the Roman Catholic Church (and, in the Greek Orthodox faith, under the name of the Feast of the Falling Asleep of Our Lady, the Most Holy Theotokos) on the 15th of August. Sources for belief in the Assumption were first credited by Gregory of Tours, but the festival, according to historical reports, was not universally celebrated until the seventh century. After the Reformation reformed churches rejected the celebration of the Assumption.

St. Athanasius: Patriarch of Alexandria in the fourth century, and one of the four great Fathers of the Eastern Church. Athanasius was many times driven from his charge but steadfastly fought against the heresies and corruptions of his time. The Creed of Athanasius, relating the mystery of the Holy Trinity, was probably compiled during the fifth century. St. Athanasius' feast day is celebrated May 2nd.

Atonement: The Day of Atonement, or *Yom Kippur,* which see.

Auckland: The provincial district of Auckland, New Zea-

land, celebrates its anniversary on the 29th of January, or
the Monday nearest that date. The city of Auckland was
founded in 1840 as the original capital of New Zealand.

Audubon: See Bird Day.

St. Augustine: Born in Africa in 354, Augustine was saved
from the profligacy of his early life by Manichaean teachings
and from this heresy by Bishop Ambrose of Milan. After several years of monastic discipline Augustine entered the priesthood in 391. Because of his strength of personality and great
learning he was elected to the bishopric of Hippo only five
years later, with dominion over most of Roman Christian
Africa. Aurelius Augustine is not to be confused with the
Archbishop of Canterbury appointed by Gregory I. in 596. St.
Aurelius Augustine is one of the four great Latin Fathers of
the Church. His feast day is the 28th of August. The feast day
of St. Augustine of Canterbury, Apostle of the English who
was charged with evangelizing England in the sixth century,
is celebrated on the 26th of May.

Auld Deer: February 16th was for centuries the date of the
old Scottish Cattle Fair, a popular day for weather prognostication in Scotland, and the feast day of an obscure "saint,"
Auld Deer, from whom the name is derived.

Ausschiesset: The annual Shooting Festival held at Tun,
Switzerland, in October. The occasion commemorates Wil-
liam Tell's killing of the Austrian leader Gessler, and the
Battle of Morat of 1476.

Australia: National celebration of Australia's founding
day became general throughout the several states by 1890:
in 1935 the title "Australia Day" supplanted the terms "Victoria Day" and "Anniversary Day." Australia Day is observed
on January 26th or the nearest Monday following.

Awakeners: The Day of the Awakeners, or the Denna
Buditelite, which see.

Azereth: Observed by conservative and Orthodox Jews for
two days immediately following the Feast of the Booths.

The Festival of Azereth, or *Shemini Azereth* as it is called
in the Bible (Deut. 16:8), includes preparation for and celebration of the ceremony known as *Succoth* or Rejoicing in

the Law (which see). The festival falls in the latter half of October, on the 23rd day of Tishri, the first civil month of the Jewish calendar.

Bairam: See *Ramadan.*

Baisakhi: Hindu New Year. See *Hindu Holidays.*

Bali Worship: The fourth day of the Hindu Garland of Lights or Diwali, at which time sacred animals are paraded through the village streets. Bali Worship Day commemorates an ancient battle between castes.

Bank Holidays: Since all parties are by law exempted from presentation or payment on legal holidays, Sundays and half-day Saturdays, the term has a semi-legal connotation, though in slang it may refer to any legal holiday. While official holidays in the United States are established by gubernatorial action for individual states, bank holidays in England were established in 1871 by Parliamentary action. They include Easter Monday, Whitmonday, the first Monday in August, Boxing Day, and December 26th.

Banners: *Tango-no-Sekku* falls on the fifth day of the fifth month in Japan. Each household which can boast of a male child displays on this occasion a brightly colored paper fish, one for each child, on a bamboo pole. The fish, representing a carp, is symbolic of good health and long life. See also Hina-no-Sekku, Japanese girls' day.

St. Barbara: The feast day, the 4th of December, of St. Barbara is, in many parts of central Europe, regarded as the beginning of the Christmas season. Memory of the virgin Barbara, martyred under the persecution of Maximinus in 306, was brought from the Middle East by the Crusaders, and she was regarded as patron saint of all persons imprisoned in fortresses. Because of the flash of lightning which, by tradition, is reputed to have killed her father when he himself dragged her before her accusers, she is also regarded as patroness of those who work with fire, including cooks, beacon and light crews, and artillery soldiers. Miners also chose St. Barbara to intercede for them.

St. Barnabas: Feast day of St. Barnabas, sponsor of St. Paul at Jerusalem, is observed in Latin churches on the 11th

of June. In the Greek Orthodox Church both St. Bartholomew's
and St. Barnabas' feast days are celebrated together on this
date. Barnaby's Day, as the occasion was called in England,
had a greater popularity before the change of calendar style,
especially among the clergy and novitiate.

St. Bartholomew: The 24th of August is celebrated as
Feast day of St. Bartholomew, one of the twelve apostles.
When traveling on a mission in Armenia, Bartholomew suf-
fered martyrdom by being flayed alive. His emblem is a
knife, the instrument of his torture. His earlier name was
Nathaniel.

Basanta: A spring festival day in India. On Basanta, which
in Sanskrit means "yellow," the sacred color of Hindu India,
the goddess Saraswati is remembered with fasting and prayer.
Saraswati, goddess of the sixty-four arts and sciences, is wife
of the great Brahma; the significance of Basanta is primarily
cultural and artistic. In a popular sense it marks the approach
of the Holi Festival, which comes three weeks later.

St. Basil: The Roman Church commemorates the Feast of
St. Basil on June 14, the Greek Orthodox Church on the first
day of the year. One of the most ascetic of the saints, St.
Basil the Great effected important changes in monastic life
and liturgy, especially of the Eastern Church. In Russia and
throughout the Levant, St. Basil was a popular saint, roughly
comparable to St. Nicholas. St. Basil's Eve required special
preparation, by the children, with traditional cakes and
songs.

Bastille: Historically, the anniversary of the fall of the
Bastille celebrates the end of an era of class privilege and
lettres de cachet, the beginning of the French Revolution.
But the significance of the event has meaning for many
countries. In France, Bastille Day, the 14th of July, is a
national holiday, in Paris especially a great celebration known
as the *Fête Nationale,* which is marked by processions and
dancing.

Bean-Throwing Night: See *Setsubun,* Japanese Spring Festival.

St. Bede: May 27th was declared the feast day of the "Venerable Bede" (*Baeda venerabilis*) when this important historical figure was elevated, by Leo XIII in 1899 to the position of a Catholic saint. Bede's *Ecclesiastical History of the English People* and missionary work among the British tribes make him one of the most important figures of his time (672-735).

Beginning-of-Work See *Shigoto Hajime,* Japanese Festival analogous to Plough Monday.

Beheading: The Feast of the Beheading, the 29th of August, is the second festival celebrated in the Oriental Church in honor of the Glorious Forerunner, John the Baptist. This day, strictly observed as an important fast day on the Greek Orthodox calendar, is somewhat less important in the Latin Church.

Belgium: Leopold I ascended the throne of Belgium on July 21, 1831, the anniversary date of Belgium's independence from the Netherlands, as *Dag der Nationale Onafhanke'yheid.*

St. Benedict: The feast day of St. Benedict of Nursia (480?-543) is celebrated, in the Western Church, on the 21st of March. St. Benedict, Abbot, and founder of the Benedictine order, may be considered the father of monasticism in the West.

Bennington Battle: The 16th of August is a state holiday in Vermont, especially remembered in Bennington where, in 1777, General Stark won a striking victory over British forces near the site of this city.

St. Bernadette: See Our Lady of Lourdes.

Bija Mangala (or Phut Mongkhon): April 15th. This rite marks the commencement of the cultivation of the fields.

Bird: Celebrated also under the name of Audubon Day, it is largely through the good services of Audubon Societies throughout this country that this day is, in most states, set aside in the interest of protecting our bird life. New York celebrates Arbor Day and Bird Day on the second Friday in April.

Birthday of the Sun and Moon: The traditional celebrations, in China, on the second day of the Second Moon, and on the fifteenth day of the Eighth Moon. See *T'ai Yang* and *T'ai Yin*.

Black Friday: The name given to two memorable dates in the financial history of the United States. The first, September 24, 1869, marked the crisis precipitated by Jay Gould and James Fisk, Jr.; the second, September 19, 1873, marked the beginning of the panic of that year.

Good Friday has also been called Black Friday because on that day church altars are covered in black and black vestments are worn by the clergy.

Black Monday: The term applied to Easter Monday and, in England to the Easter Monday of April, 1360, when Edward II's troops perished outside Paris.

St. Blaise: The feast day (the 3rd of February) of this early martyr was especially popular in Europe during the Middle Ages. Blaise, a fourth-century bishop in Armenia, was invoked as a helper in sickness, especially for throat ailments. In England he was adopted as patron saint of the wool combers. Towns in which this industry flourished during the eighteenth century were accustomed to holding spectacles in honor of Jason and the Golden Fleece and St. Blaise.

Blowing of the Trumpet: *Rosh-Ha-shanah* or The Day of Blowing of the Trumpet is the first day of the Jewish religious new year, also called the Day of Judgment. See *Rosh Hashanah*.

Blue Monday: At one time the name given the Monday before Lent when Christian churches were decorated in blue. On this day certain labors were excused from work. The day was also called Saint Monday.

Bobby Burns: See *Burns*.

Bodhi: Anniversary of the establishment of Buddhism as a world religion. On the day of the full moon in the month of Vaisakha Lord Buddha devoted himself to attaining enlightenment. The name "Bodhi" associated with his decision refers to the Bodhi tree at Budhagaya, India, where Buddha attained enlightenment. Bodhi Day is generally observed on December 7, or the Sunday nearest that date.

Bolivia: Bolivia's independence from Peru is celebrated on August 6th; it was declared in 1825. See *Bolivar*.

Bolivar: The anniversary of the birth of Simon Bolivar, national patriot of Venezuela, is celebrated on July 24th throughout most South American countries. Bolivar, by his energy, diplomacy and wisdom, not only gained Venezuela's independence (in 1811) but laid the foundation for the Pan-American Union itself. Bolivar was active in securing freedom for Bolivia, Colombia, Ecuador and Peru, and, indirectly, helped other republics as well.

Bon: A Buddhist festival in Japan. The Bon Festival is presumed to have begun in 657. Each week in July Japanese dancers celebrate the joyful entry of their loved ones into Paradise.

St. Boniface: Feast day of St. Boniface falls on the 5th of June, in anniversary of his martyrdom. Boniface—born Winfrith (or Winfrid) in Devonshire, England—served most of his adult years as a missionary to Germanic tribes in central Europe. Gregory II conferred this name and the title of bishop upon him in 723; later, under Gregory III, Boniface was made archbishop to the Germans.

Book Week: Originating in 1919, Book Week has had some success under the sponsorship of Book Week Headquarters, an American organization which seeks to assure special interest in books during the middle week in November.

Boone: Kentucky has, following the two hundredth anniversary of the death of Daniel Boone, in 1934, given special programs on this day, June 7th, generally under the auspices of the Kentucky State Historical Society.

Booth: Booth: See *Salvation Army*.

Booths: For the Jewish Feast of Booths, see *Tabernacles*.

Boris: January 30th was formerly observed in honor of the birth of Rozhden Den na Tzar Boris III, King of the Bulgarians (born 1894). The fete also paid tribute to Boris I, whose great influence, conversion to Christianity and establishment of the Eastern Church gave spiritual life to Bulgaria.

Boston Tea Party: Anniversary of the celebrated "tea

party," during which the colonists showed their displeasure at taxes imposed on imports of tea from England. In 1773 two ships attempted to break the embargo which the colonists had placed on their cargo. On December 16 these ships were boarded by a company of men dressed as Indians, and the cargo was thrown into the sea. The occasion is marked by patriotic observances under local rather than national or state auspices.

Boxing: An English and Dominion holiday, on December 26th, Boxing Day, the first day after Christmas, otherwise known as St. Stephen's Day. Presumably the day derives its popular appelation from Christmas boxes of clothes, food and gratuities which formerly were distributed among employees, tradespeople, public servants and menials. The occasion in modern England is principally remembered because it marks the beginning of the Pantomimes, which last until Lent.

Boy Scouts of America: February 8th is the birthday of the founding of the Boy Scout movement in America. Begun in England by Lord Baden-Powell, the movement was carried to the United States by Dan Beard, who established the organization here in 1910. February 8th begins or is included in National Boy Scout Week.

Boyaca: The Anniversary of the Battle of Boyaca, August 7, 1819. On this date Bolivar defeated the Spanish Army and so obtain Colombia's complete independence from Spain. The anniversary may be considered analagous to the Fourth of July in the United States.

Boyne: For anniversary of the Batle of Boyne. See *Orange Day*.

Brazil: Brazil's independence from Spanish rule in 1822 is celebrated September 7th.

St. Bridget: Feast day of St. Bridget (or St. Bride) who, with St. Patrick, is spiritual patron of Ireland, is celebrated February 1st. By tradition Bridget, daughter of a pre-Christian Ulster chieftain, made herself a nun's cell in a great oak tree (literally a *Kil-dara* or "cell of the oak") about the

year 585. The city of Kildare was built around this site. St.
Bridget founded the first nunnery in Ireland and, in Ireland, is remembered as the nuns' "spiritual mother."

Brotherhood Week: Sponsored by the National Conference of Christians and Jews in the United States, this week
begins annually on Washington's Birthday.

Buart Nark: The Buddhist ordination ceremony, most frequently celebrated in the spring, during which time young
Thai men are taken into the priesthood. Since each young
man of Thailand is expected to become a monk, if only for
a short time, the ceremony is a national as well as religious
holiday.

Buddha Vaisakha Purnima: Birthday of the Lord Buddha
in India, called Wesak Day in Japan. Indian Buddhists and
many non-Buddhists participate in this annual celebration in
honor of the princely Gautama in late April or May. The
most famous of these takes place at Budha-Gaya in the province of Hihar, India, where Buddha received enlightenment.

Buddy Week: See *Poppy Week.*

Bulgaria: *Den na Nezavisimost'ta,* observed March 3rd, is
the anniversary of Bulgaria's freedom from Turkish rule, by
Treaty of San Stefano in 1887.

Bunker Hill: Usually celebrated as a bank holiday in Boston. Bunker Hill Day commemorates the heroism shown by
American troops defeated in the battle there on June 17, 1775.

Burbank: For Luther Burbank's birthday, see *Arbor Day.*

Burns: "Bobby" Burns' birthday on January 25th is one
of the most important holidays for the Scottish, who traditionally have gathered to celebrate the occasion and sing the
songs of their beloved poet. Curiously, Burns himself, writing
to a friend, claimed that "you may henceforth expect to see
my birthday inscribed among the wonderful events, in the
Poor Robin and Aberdeen Almanacks, along with the Black
Monday and the Battle of Bothwell-bridge."

Butter Week: In old Russia the week preceding Lent was
popularly known as *Maslyanitza,* "Butter Week." In the Western church called "Carnival," it corresponded to the carnival

spirit which prevailed at that time throughout Europe. The week presumably derived its Russian name from the fine pastries prepared for the occasion.

Caedmon: Caedmon, most ancient of English bards, was recognized a saint by the Anglo-Saxon Church. February 11, 680 was determined the day of his death, and this day was later observed as St. Caedmon's Day by the Roman Church in Britain.

Calendar: See *New Year.*

Candlemas: Otherwise called the Purification of the Virgin or the Purification of Mary, an important Christian holiday celebrated on February 2nd, forty days after Christmas. In Roman Catholic and Anglican churches candles are distributed to the worshipers. These, in Rome, are carried in procession on Candlemass, Annunciation, Assumption, and the Feast of the Nativity of Mary. Candlemass appears to have been introduced into Western Christianity about the seventh century; it corresponds to and, indeed, grew out of Eastern observances of Christ's Presentation in the Temple. (February 2nd is observed in the Greek Orthodox and Coptic churches as the anniversary of the Presentation.) Perhaps because of the similarity between the month and Februation, purification rites associated with the Roman Lupercalia, it was for a time believed that the Christian ceremonies had a pagan origin, but scholars now believe otherwise.

During the Middle Ages Candlemas was rent-paying day; it was also considered an excellent time for forecasting the weather. Popular custom in America still tells of the ground hog looking for his shadow on February 2nd.

Candy: From the Turkish term for Candy, *"Id-al-Fitr,"* the three day feast which marks the end of Ramadan. See *Id-al-Fitr* and *Ramadan.*

Canterbury: The Provincial District of Canterbury, New Zealand, celebrates a territorial anniversary on the 16th of December or on the Monday nearest that date.

St. Canute: "Cnute the Great," King of Norway, Denmark and England. He was born in 995 and made his great invasion of England in 1015. His reign greatly extended the rule

of his Scandinavian people and was characterized by order
and good government. His feast day is celebrated Jan. 19th.
The feast day of St. Canute, Martyr, is celebrated Jan. 7th and
marks the end of the Christmas holidays in Sweden.

Carleton: Will Carleton's Birthday, October 21st, was set
aside for special observance in the state of Michigan in the
year 1923. Will Carleton's poems include "Over the Hill to
the Poor House" and "Out of the Old House, Nancy."

Carling Sunday: The fifth Sunday in Lent, so called from
the tradition of eating specially prepared peas or "carlings"
on this occasion. The term is almost exclusively English. In
the north of England the fourth Sunday in Lent, otherwise
known as "mothering Sunday," was called Carling Sunday. On
this occasion children would prepare cakes and presents for
their mothers.

Carmine: The annual celebration of the Festival of the
Madonna del Carmine, patron saint of Naples, is widely
known throughout Europe and America. It falls on July 16th.

Carnation: The first celebration of the birth of our twenty-
fifth President, William McKinley, received popular impetus
in 1903 with the formation of the Carnation League. This
organization enlisted the support of the President, governors
and senators of several states, and the people, to arouse party
interest in political activities. It took as its emblem the carnation, the beloved President's favorite flower. Carnation Day,
January 29th, was popular for several years.

Carnival: Literally *carnivale*, "farewell to flesh," Carnival
is the name given, in Roman Catholic countries, to the three
days immediately preceding Lent, from Epiphany to Ash
Wednesday, a time given over to feasting and revelry. By
association it has come to refer to any occasion officially given
over to merrymaking. Most states and several cities of the
United States have an official Carnival Season, of which the
Mardi Gras, the New Orleans carnival established in 1830, is
perhaps the best-known.

Carp-Flying: See *Tango-No-Sekku*, the Japanese Boys' Festival.

St. Catherine: Feast day of St. Catherine of Alexandria, patroness of wheelwrights, mechanics, and philosophers, comes on the 25th of November. Catherine is said to have vanquished the Roman Emperor Maximianus in argument and to have destroyed, through her prayers, the great spiked wheel which he had ordered built for her to be tortured on. Her feast day, the last holy day before Advent, was a popular date, during the Middle Ages, for weddings. The more famous Catherine of Catholic martyrology, however, is St. Catherine of Siena, who played an active political role during the fourteenth century, especially at Pisa and Florence, in support of the Pope. Her feast day is celebrated April 30th.

Chair of St. Peter: St. Peter's establishment of the see of Antioch is observed by the Roman Church as St. Peter's Chair at Antioch, on Feb. 22nd. St. Peter's establishment of the see of Rome, commemorating the primacy of Rome, is observed on Jan. 18th. Since 1910 St. Peter's Chair at Rome has marked the beginning of the Chair of Unity Octave (ending with the Conversion of St. Paul), with special prayers for the unity of all people of the Church of Rome.

Chakri: On April 6th, Chakri Day in Thailand, the Royal Pantheon is opened to crowds who come to pay homage to the ancestors of the royal family, specifically to the statues of eight kings of the present dynasty.

Change of Style: George II of England signed the act by which England adopted the calendar that Pope Gregory had, in the sixteenth century, formalized in central Europe. This act provided that the legal year should, in 1752, begin on January 1st, and that the eleven days between the third and fourteenth of September should that year be dropped from the calendar. Thus, while January 14th was New Year's Day, Old Style, the calendar which we now know made the first of the month New Year's Day, New Style. For more details, see *New Year.*

Charles I: The martyrdom of the Blessed King Charles I, beheaded on January 30, 1649, was greatly venerated by Tories and followers of the Pretenders, both in England and the colonies. By an act of the General Assembly of Virginia this day was set aside for special mourning throughout that colony, and the tradition was continued, in one form or another, for many years after the Federation.

Cherokee Strip: The "Cherokee Outlet"—over six million acres of Tonkawa and Pawnee land in northern Oklahoma— was opened for white settlement on September 16, 1893. The anniversary of this date is remembered as Cherokee Strip Day, an optional legal holiday in the state of Oklahoma.

Cherry Blossom: The events and festivals of Japan which are connected with the Viewing of the Cherry Blossoms are many and varied, but they included, in the old regime, a special imperial party for this occasion.

Chi Hsi: The Chinese "Festival of the Milky Way," Chi Hsi marks the occasion when, this one time in the year, the star Vega joins her husband Aquila on the other side of the Milky Way, which separates them. It falls on the seventh day of the Seventh Moon and is known also as "Threading the Needle Holiday" or "Festival of Tragic Lovers."

In Japan the Feast of Tanabata commemorates the same morphological story; it too is celebrated on the seventh day of the Seventh Moon and is, like Chi Hsi, a festival for women.

The story related in China on the classical stage tells of the love of Altair and Vega. Altair, disguised as a shepherd, saw Vega as she left her heavenly loom to bathe in an earthly stream. Because the lovers neglected their heavenly duties, they were forced to live on opposite sides of the river, the Milky Way, except for this one night of the year.

Chicago Fire: October 9th is the anniversary of the great fire in Chicago which in 1871 destroyed a large part of the city. It has, in recent years, been the occasion for public-spirited gatherings in that city and for political and local celebrations.

Child Health: Authorized by Congress in 1928, Child Health Day was observed by gubernatorial proclamation in most states on May 1, 1929, and for some years thereafter.

Childermas: See *Holy Innocents' Day*, the Christian feast day on December 28th commemorating Herod's slaughter of all male children in Bethlehem.

Children's: The second Sunday in June has, since 1868, been observed, by Protestant churches in the United States, as Children's Day.

Ch'ing Ming: Exactly one hundred and six days after the winter solstice a second spring festival, called Ch'ing Ming, is celebrated in China. This "Pure and Bright Festival," involving three days of preparation during which time the fires are allowed to go out so that they may be lit again, is essentially a First Feast of the Dead. At this time the dead are honored, the graves decorated with willow twigs, and offerings made both to ancestors and the gods. Ch'ing Ming is preceded by Li Chum, the "Promise-of-Spring Festival."

Christmas: Literally, Christ's Mass, the celebration of the birth of Christ, the greatest of the Christian holy days. The date of December 25th was, presumably, established by Pope Julius I in the first half of the fourth century; since this time both Eastern and Western churches have agreed to celebrate Christmas at the same time. Before this agreement, however, the lack of uniformity in observance permitted some confusion between Christian rites and popular pagan festivals of the winter solstice. Traditions from the Gothic *Jule* (Yule) may still be noted in the secularized celebration of Christmas.

St. Christopher: St. Christopher, patron saint of travel and protector against storms and accidents, is especially remembered on the 25th of July. While himself a very obscure saint who suffered martyrdom under Decius in the third century, romance associated with his name has made him into an enormous man who carried people across a stream on his shoulders and once carried Christ in this same manner.

Chrysanthemums: A Japanese festival celebrating, in modern times on the 9th of October, the joy and beauty of flowers and especially of chrysanthemums. From this festival we derive our annual chrysanthemum and dahlia shows in the West.

Ch'u Hsi: The Night of the Thirtieth, New Year's Eve in China, is analogous to our own New Year's Eve. It occurs the night of the twenty-ninth day of the Twelfth Moon. Family observances, collection of old debts and general rejoicing make it one of the most festive occasions of the year. Comparable to the Japanese *Omisoka*. (See *Yüan Tan*, New Year's Day.)

Ch'ung Yang Chieh: The Chinese Festival of High Places or Kite Flying Festival is a special holiday for men and boys. It is celebrated on the ninth day of the Ninth Month. On this day many-shaped kites are flown from the heights in honor of the escape from danger of one Fei Ch'ung-yang, who fled to a high place.

Ch'u Yuan: The Chinese festival of Tang Wu is one of three annual occasion of settling accounts. It falls on the fifth day of the Fifth Moon. Originally meant to honor Ch'u Yüan, principal patriot of the Chou dynasty, the day is observed by dragon-boat racing and often called by his name. For twenty-three hundred years dragon boats have each year raced to a designated place in the river to be the first to offer rice and sweets to the departed spirit of Ch'u Yüan. The day also provides a special occasion for incurring the favor of the dragon spirit, the principle of beneficience in nature, of spring and rain. See *Dead*.

Cinco De Mayo: The Fifth of May, a day of popular and patriotic observance in Mexico and by Mexicans in the United States. The Fifth of May celebrates the Batle of Guadalupe in 1862, at which a small Mexican force defeated a French army three times its size, proving themselves capable of successfully resisting foreign invasion.

Circumcision: Among the Jews a rite instituted by God and enjoined upon Abraham as token of the covenant between God and His people. The act was usually performed eight days after birth. For other nations also the practice has religious significance, principally among the Mohammedans, Arabs, Fijians and Samoans as well as certain African tribes.

The Roman Christian church began, as early as 487, to celebrate January 1st as the feast day in commemoration of Christ's circumcision; the Anglican Church adopted this celebration in 1549.

Circus: Specifically, a building for exhibiting major holiday chariot races and other amusements, the term came to refer to the great Roman holidays themselves. The Roman circus, the one public festivity which both men and women might attend, was raced on the following festivals: the Consualia, the Equiria, the Ludi Romani, Ludi Plebeii, the Cerialia, Ludi Apollinares, Ludi Megalenses, and Floralia. As many as twenty-four races might take place the same day. The greatest circus, in Rome, was the Circus Maximus, several times rebuilt and elegantly furnished.

St. Cnute: See *St. Canute.*

Cobblers' Holiday: Folk name for Monday. By popular folklore, probably of the twelfth or thirteenth century, cobblers and shoemakers took Monday as their special holiday. (It was customary during the late Middle Ages for each craft or guild to receive one day each week as a holiday.)

Cold Food Days: See *Han Shih.*

Collop Monday: The Monday before Shrove Tuesday, the day on which, traditionally, faithful Christians should stop eating collops, or flesh meat. Also the days of merrymaking which were associated with this carnival occasion. Because of the numerous poems written in honor of the reigning pagan spirit customary before penence, the day was also known, in England and parts of late medieval Europe, as Poets' Day, or Poets' Monday.

Colorado: August 1st, the anniversary of Colorado's admission into the Union one hundred years after the signing of the Declaration of Independence. A state holiday in Colorado.

Columbus: In honor of the four-hundredth anniversary of Columbus' discovery of America, President Benjamin Harrison declared the 12th of October a general holiday for the year 1892. It is at present celebrated in all but thirteen states. Since the Columbian Exposition held in Chicago in 1893 to mark the same anniversary of the discovery, countries of the Pan American Union, together with the United States and Canada, have given this day official recognition. In some states Columbus Day is known as Discovery Day. See also *Race Day.*

Commonwealth: In Puerto Rico July 25th is celebrated as the anniversary of the island's free association with the United

States. It is called Commonwealth Day, commemorating the independence granted Puerto Rico in 1952.

Communion Sunday: World-Wide Communion Sunday, the first Sunday in October, is sponsored by the Federated Council of the Churches of Christ in America.

Conception of St. Anne: Meaning, St. Anne conceived Mary: see *Immaculate Conception.*

Conception of John the Baptist: Celebrated on the 24th of September, this was the third festival formerly observed by the Oriental Christian Church in honor of St. John the Baptist. It commemorated the angelic announcement of his birth. The nativity of John the Baptist, his beheading and his baptism of Christ provide the occasions for other feast days associated with his name. See *John the Baptist.*

Confederate Memorial: Nine states of the Confederacy do not celebrate Memorial Day on May 30, but prefer the 26th of August. Alabama, Florida, Georgia and Mississippi observe August 26th, while North and South Carolina prefer May 10th, and Tennessee June 13th.

Confucius: The birthday of Confucius is celebrated the twenty-eighth day of the Eighth Moon in China. This beloved Chinese teacher and philosopher, who for centuries has influenced men's thoughts, gathered together most of what we know of earlier writings of the feudal period.

Constitution: The anniversary of the signing of the Constitution of the United States, on September 17, 1787, has been observed in various cities and by public-spirited organizations throughout the country, with fitting ceremonies The American Bar Association has been particularly active in urging more states to preserve the dignity of this occasion.

In most democratic countries Constitution Day is celebrated as a national holiday, especially in northern European countries.

Conversion of St. Paul: The Catholic festival of gratitude for St. Paul's miraculous conversion was instituted in the Western Christian churches some time during the eighth or ninth century. It is celebrated on January 25th and marks the end of the Chair of Unity Octave. (See St. Peter's Chair). Since medieval times St. Paul's Day has been a popular occasion for weather prognostication.

Coronation: In certain countries (notably Jordan where, in recent years both the coronation of King Feisal I and King Hussein I have been celebrated on the anniversary of March 8th and May 2nd respectively) Coronation Day has become an annual national holiday.

Corpus Christi: The popular English and Spanish name for the *Festum Sanctissimi Corporis Christi,* Feast of the Most Holy Body of Christ. Corpus Christi was instituted at the suggestion of St. Juliana, Prioress of Mont Cornillon, in Belgium, in 1258. Established in 1264 by Pope Urban IV as a festival in honor of the Holy Eucharist and reasserted by Pope Clement V in 1314, the splendor and solemnity of the occasion became popular throughout the Western Church, and were later adopted by many sects of the Eastern Church. Popularly named *Fronleichman* in German, *Boze Telo* in Slavic, and *'id el-jessed el-ilahi* in Arabic, Chorpus Christi is celebrated the Thursday after Trinity Sunday.

Costilla: The anniversary of Father Miguel Hidalgo y Costilla's *"grito."*

Covenant: The Union of South Africa celebrates Covenant Day on December 16th. On this day in 1838 a Boer Army under Andries Pretorius fought the Zulu forces of Dingaan, their leader, at the River Umslatos, afterward called Blood River. The firearms of the white settlers utterly defeated the natives in the first major white victory and reprisal action in Zulu territory. Also called Pretorius Day by the Boers.

St. Crispin: While there are a number of saints by this name, the feast of St. Crispin, a Roman who made shoes at night to support his missionary work in Gaul, was popular as far back as the ninth century. St. Crispin, patron of shoemakers, sadlers and tanners, was beheaded c.285 in the reign of Diocletian. In England the anniversary of the Battle of Agincourt, which falls on St. Crispin day (October 25th), lends historical significance to the occasion.

St. Cyril and Methodius: On the 24th of May Bulgarians celebrate the saint day of the two brothers who in 855 invented the alphabet which made possible a Bulgarian national language and culture.

Czechoslovakia: October 28, 1918, the day of the founding of the Czechoslovakian republic.

Daft Days: Scotch term for the Christmas holidays.

St. David: On March 1st the Welsh honor David, titular saint and last native prince of Wales, by wearing a leek, as the Irish wear green to commemorate St. Patrick's Day.

Davis: For birthday of Jefferson Davis, see *Jefferson Davis*.

Day of Wreaths: Popular term in central Europe and France for Corpus Christi. On this day great flowered wreaths are borne along the street in procession.

Dead: Special rites which pay homage to the dead are of ancient origin. The Christian Church has appointed two services, All Saints' and All Souls' Day, November 1st and 2nd, both of which fall within one of the periods of celebration memorable in pagan tradition. Visiting the graves of the departed is still, in central and eastern Europe, considered a sacred obligation, peculiar to this occasion. In many areas All Soul's Day is called the Day of the Dead (Mexico's *Dia de Muertos* is a national holiday, for instance). Especially in the Eastern Church, in Rumania, Czechoslovakia and the Balkan countries certain days for honoring the dead are kept during the Lenten season or immediately after Easter. See also *Ch'u Yüan*.

Death of General Mameo: See *Maceo*.

Death of the Liberator: The 17th of December recalls the memory of Simon Bolivar and is fittingly observed in many South American countries, especially by the Sociedad Bolivariana.

Decoration: Also called Memorial Day, a U. S. national holiday observed in many states on May 30th as an occasion for honoring those who have died in defense of this country. It was inaugurated at the close of the Civil War, by Gen. John A. Logan, Commander of the Grand Army of the Republic, who ordered that soldiers' graves be decorated with flowers and flags on this day. Decoration day remains in some measure true to its origin in the Union Army (1868). Of the ten original Confederate states, only Virginia celebrates Memorial Day. See *Confederate Memorial Day*.

Dedication: Hanukkah, or the Feast of Dedication, is an important Jewish festival celebrated for eight days in the interlunar month of Kislev, falling in December. See *Hanukkah*.

De Diego: Jose de Diego, patriot and national hero of Puerto Rico, is honored on the island on the anniversary of his birthday, April 16th.

Deepavali: Preferred Celonese spelling for Diwali, the Hindu Festival of Lights.

Defenders: A state holiday in Maryland on September 12th, honoring the defenders of Ft. McHenry during the War of 1812. See *Maryland Defenders' Day*.

De Molay: March 18th is the anniversary of the martyrdom of Jacques de Molay; the occasion is celebrated by members of the Order of de Molay, a Masonic order for boys.

Denna Buditelite: The greatest national day of the Bulgarians. It honored Christo Botev and other patriots who first awoke the nation to a spirit of unity and independence. Christo Botev is considered the finest poet writing in the Bulgarian language.

Destruction of the Temple: Four periods of fasting, which date from the Babylonian captivity, relate to the Destruction of the Temple in Jerusalem. Jewish tradition has outlined the Fast of the Tenth Month, on the tenth of Tebeth, commemorating the beginning of the seige by Nebuchadnezzar; the Fast of the Fourth Month, on the seventeenth of Tammuz, remembering the first breach in the city's walls; the Fast of the Fifth Month, in the ninth of Ab (which see), relating to the destruction of the temple; and the Fast of the Seventh Month, on the third of Tishri, commemorating the assasination of Gedaliah's Babylonian governor. Roman occupation of the city and subsequent destruction of the Temple in the year 70 c.e. is also remembered on the Seventeenth of Tammuz and the ninth of Ab respectively. (For further comment on individual fasts look at the name of Jewish month in which each falls.)

Dew Grows Cold: The Chinese festival of Han Lu, which marks the passing of summer. See *Han Lu*.

Dhana Trayodashi: The Hindu holiday celebrating the new year of the autumn season, sometimes called the New Year of Business. Dhana Trayodashi falls on the first day of Diwali festivities, or the Festival of the Garland of Lights. See *Hindu Holidays*.

Dhvajoropana: The Hindu holiday celebrating the greatest of Hindu new year seasons, the spring season. This is the chief of four Hindu New Year celebrations, each marking the commencement of a new season. It is celebrated at the time the sun enters the constellation of the House of Ares the Ram. It is also called Guddhi Padava. At this time the goddess Sitala is especially honored.

Diego: See De Diego

Dipevali: See *Diwali*, Hindu Festival of Lights.

Discovery: Variation of Columbus Day.

St. Distaff: On January 7th in England the women were used to going back to their spinning after Christmas holidays. In the uplands of England and Scotland the occasion called for much joking and many practical jokes.

Divine Mother: For the Festival of the Divine Mother, see *Durga Puja*, a ten-day holiday in India. See also *Ram Lila*.

Diwali: (In Sanskrit, Dipevali; variation, Deepavali.) Literally, a Festival of Lights, taking its name from the main feature of this Indian new year celebration at which lights, candles and lamps are lavishly used. Historically the event is associated with the coronation of Vikramaditya, the first Gupta king. The day commemorates one of four new years celebrated in India.

Beginning on the new moon of Karttika, in our month of October or November, Diwali is celebrated for five days in the autumn. The first of these days commemorates Dhana Trayodashi, the New Year of Business, the new year of the autumn season; the second, the triumph of the God Vishnu over Narakasura; the third, the virtues of Lakshmi, Vishnu's wife; the fourth, Bali Worship Day (which see) and the last Yama holiday (which see). Diwali is also a holiday honoring the moon, when sacred cows and bulls are worshiped. It falls in October or November, by the Gregorian calendar.

Doctors: March 30th has been designated as Doctors' Day throughout the state of Louisiana, in honor of the medical profession of this state.

Doleing: Alternate name for St. Thomas's Day, which see.

Doljatra-Swing: In Bengal, India, the name given to Holi, the great Hindu carnival. At this festival (in March) swings are made for the images of the Lord Krishna and Radha, Divine Lovers.

Dolls: For the Japanese Feast of Dolls, see *Hina-no-Sekku.*

St. Dominic: August 4th is the feast day of Dominic de Guzman, who was canonized by Gregory IX in 1234 for his purposeful devotion to the welfare of others and for his establishment of the order (sanctioned in 1215) of the Dominicans.

Dominion: The Canadian celebration of Dominion Day on July 1st roughly corresponds to our Fourth of July; it marks the anniversary of Parliament's passing the North American Act of 1867 by which all Canadian colonies were united under one confederation and Canada became a free and independent Dominion of the British Empire.

Dragon Boat Festival: See *Ch'u Yüan* and *Tuan Wu.*

Durga Puja: The Festival of the Divine Mother, Durga Puja, a ten-day holiday in India celebrating the creative force of the universe. The ten-armed Durga, wife of Siva, the Destroyer, is placed above all other Hindu goddesses. One of her daughters married Brahma the creator, and her husband Siva is also of the Hindu Trinity. Durga has many names. See *Hindu Holidays.* In Bengal, India, the Durga Puja is known as the Festival of Victory, the Dussehra. The Divine Mother is also known as Bhavani, Devi, Kali, Parvati, Uma, etc.

Dussehra: The Hindu Festival of Victory or *Dussehra* commemorates in October the victory of the Goddess Durga (or Kali) over the demon Mahishasura. In Bengal called Durga Puja (see above); in north and south India the festival celebrates the victory of Rama (hero of the *Ramayana*) over

Ravana, demon-king of Lanka. In essence this festival celebrates the victory of good over evil.

Easter: The Christian festival annually celebrating the
resurrection of Jesus Christ from the dead. The resurrection
and appearances play a prominent part in the New Testament (Mat. 28, Mark 16, Luke 24, John 20, 1 Cor. 15, etc.).
Easter forms one of the three great festivals of the Christian
Church, the others being Christmas and Pentecost. Lent is
the Easter season of preparation, as Advent prepares for
Christmas.

The proper date for observing Easter has caused a great
deal of controversy; originally it was reckoned the same as
the Jewish Passover. But controversies arising out of the fact
that both a lunar and a solar calendar were involved continued into modern times. The date was established by the
Council of Nicaea in 325 as the first Sunday after the full
moon on or after March 21st. The matter of the date was reconsidered in 1923 and, after that submitted to the League of
Nations, but no secularly established date was accepted. In
the United States, Easter is celebrated on the first Sunday
after the fourteenth day of the moon reigning at the Vernal
Equinox, but in England on the first Sunday after the second
Saturday in April. Many dates in the ecclesiastical calendar
are set by Easter.

The term "Easter" is derived from the name of the Teutonic goddess of spring, Eostre. Easter bonfires, especially common in Nordic countries, could probably be traced to ancient
Saxon rites. In many countries the day after Easter is reckoned
a great holiday: see especially *Anden Paäskedag*.

Easter Monday: The first day after Easter is a legal holiday in North Carolina.

Easter Week: See *Holy Week.*

Easter Weekend: The two days preceding Easter are
legal holidays in twelve states and in Puerto Rico. In California Good Friday is a legal half-holiday.

Edict of Nantes: See *Huguenot Day.*

St. Edmund: November 16th is feast day of Edmund, Archbishop of Canterbury in 1227, canonized in 1247 by Pope Innocent IV. Nov. 20th is the feast day of St. Edmund, (849-79) King of East Anglis.

Eight-Hour: Popular term which had semi-official status in New South Wales, for Australia's Labor Day. Largely supplanted by the term Six-Hour Day since, in 1948, the forty-hour week became general throughout Australia.

Eighth Moon: See *Dragon Boat Festival.*

Eisteddfod: A Welsh tradition possibly dating from the fourth century, Eisteddfod is, according to one writer, a national congress which meets annually for the encouragement of Welsh national music and literature. It is held the first week of August.

Election: General Election Day is celebrated, in the United States, the first Tuesday after the first Monday in November. Congressional action affecting the date of election came as early as 1792. The present date was established in 1845 as affecting Presidential elections, and in 1872 as affecting members of the House being elected on the same day on even or biennial years.

Elevation of the Cross: The Elevation of the Life-Giving Cross, strictly observed in the Greek Orthodox Church as a day of fasting, is more commonly called the Exaltation of the Cross or Holy Cross Day. See *Exaltation of the Cross.*

St. Elijah: The feast day of the Glorious Saint and Prophet Elijah the Thesbite, of 895 B.C., is observed by the Greek Orthodox Church on July 20th. Among the peasantry of Rumania and Lithuania this day was a time for taking special precautions against the spirits of storm and house.

Emancipation: January 1st is observed, by many people in the United States, as the anniversary of Lincoln's proclamation freeing the slaves. September 22nd is less generally observed as an anniversary of similar import, while the day is celebrated on June 19th in Texas, August 2nd in Illinois or on the date of the adoption of the Thirteenth Amendment in other states. Emancipation Day (March 22nd) is a legal holiday in Puerto Rico.

Ember: Christian ecumenical days. Particularly important Ember days are Wednesday, Friday and Saturday of each Ember week. Of the latter there are four, marking the four seasons of the year, beginning respectively on Holy Cross Day, St. Lucy's Day, the first Sunday in Lent, and Whitsunday. These weeks are set aside in the Western Church for special fasting, ordination of the clergy and prayer. Their observance was recognized throughout Europe by the eighth century. The name is derived from the Anglo-Saxon *"ymb-ren,"* meaning "circular" or "revolution."

Empire: See *Victoria Day*, May 24th, also called British Empire Day.

Eiphany: January 6th, twelve days after Christmas, is accepted by most Christian churches as the spiritual brithday or baptismal day of Christ. In the Greek Orthodox Church it is called the Holy Theophany. In the West it is celebrated also as Magi Day or the Festival of Three Kings, the Feast of Declaration, Day of Lights and Twelfth Night. Epiphany, meaning "the appearance," was celebrated at least by the second century as the occasion of Christ's baptism, but also in commemoration of the manifestation of Christ to the Gentiles —that is, to the three Magi or Wise Men of the East—and of diverse miracles which were specially remembered on this occasion.

Twelfth Night Eve was a popular occasion for rustic entertainment during the Middle Ages, and since carnival merry-making and pleasure began at Epiphany, the day had somewhat less spiritual than secular interest. See *Carnival* and *Twelfth Day*.

Equinox: Both the vernal and autumnal equinox have, more especially in ancient times, been the occasion for diverse celebrations. They occur, respectively, in late March and late September, between the 20th and 23rd of the month.

Leif Ericson: Celebrated by many Norwegians on the North American Continent in honor of the first Norse Viking, Leif Ericson, who landed at Vineland about the year 1000.

Erste Zondag: In Belgium Erste Zondag von den Vasten,

the first Sunday of Lent, great bonfires were built on the heights, much as, in England, St. John's fires on Twelfth Day Eve. See *Fires*.

Esther: The Jewish Feast of Esther is observed on the thirteenth day of the month called Adar, the sixth civil and twelfth sacred month of the Jewish calendar. Observed on the day preceding the Feast of Purim in commemoration of the fast mentioned in the Bible (Esther 9:18). Sometimes referred to as the Fast of Adar.

Etchmiadzin: The second Sunday after Pentecost is a national holiday among the Armenians, celebrated principally at the city of Etchmiadzin where, according to tradition, Christ himself appeared at the cathedral. Many pilgrimages have been made to the city, and the cathedral contains, among other sacred relics, the hand of St. Gregory.

Eucharist: In the Roman Catholic Church two great feasts commemorate the Holy Eucharist (also called Mass, the Lord's Supper, the Holy Eucharist or Holy Sacrament). These are Holy Thursday and Corpus Christi.

Evacuation: Boston annually celebrates the withdrawal of British forces on March 17, 1776. This date marked one of Washington's major victories over General Howe.

Exaltation of the Cross: The feast of the Exaltation of the Holy Cross on the 14th of September was instituted in the seventh century by the Emperor Heraclius. It celebrates the recovery of the true cross carried away from Jerusalem by Chosroes the Persian, the vision of the cross seen by Constantine in 312 (the cross appeared in the heavens with the words *"In Hoc Signo Vinces"*), and references in the New Testament (John 19 and I Corinthians 1).

This feast is also called Holy Rood (Holyrood) Day. It is celebrated in the Greek Orthodox Church as a strict fast day, in Mexico (on the 3rd of May) as the traditional festival of bricklayers. See *Invention of the Cross*.

Falling Asleep of Our Lady: The Feast of the Falling Asleep of Our Lady, the Most Holy Theotokos, celebrated on the 15th of August in the Greek Orthodox Church, called Assumption in Western Christian churches. (*See Assumption*.)

Fascism: The anniversary of the founding of the Fascistic state in Italy was observed, under Mussolini's direction and during his lifetime, on March 23rd.

Fast: The first Monday in April is still observed by many people in New Hampshire as a holiday. First official record of this holiday was date 1679. New Hampshire is the only state to keep this holiday, though the manner of observance has changed through the years.

Fastern's E'en: North of England and Scotch local term for Shrove Tuesday.

Father of Texas: Stephen Fuller Austin, the "Father of Texas," is honored in his state on the 30th of November.

Father's: As the name indicates, a day on which fathers are particularly remembered with gifts and cards. Adopted shortly after Mother's Day became a national custom. Mrs. John Bruce Dodd, of Spokane, Washington, was principally responsible for the institution's success. Father's Day is a legal holiday in Arizona, on the third Sunday in June.

Fiestas Patrias: Mexico's Festival of Independence is celebrated on September 15th and 16th. In 1821 the Treaty of Córdoba granted Mexico independence. After a short period as an empire under Iturbide, a federal constitution was adopted.

Fifth Month Fast: See *Ab*, the fast of the ninth of Ab.

Finding of the Cross: The Invention (Discovery) of the Cross by Emperess Helena, mother of Constantine the Great, about 305 is commemorated on May 3rd. See *Invention of the Cross*.

Fire Festival: See Basanta, spring festival in India.

Firecracker: Popular term in some parts of the U.S. for the Fourth of July.

Fires: Fire may have a variety of associations with holiday functions. The most traditional, however, are those of the summer and winter solstice, the first giving many countries the tradition of building St. John's Fires, the latter of the Yule log burned at Christmas. In Italy bonfires (*vampate*) are lit in the squares at the Feast of the Immaculate Conception, December 8th. In England farmers once built great bonfires atop the hills on Twelfth Day Eve, January 5th, similar to those which Czechoslovakian peasants kindled to drive away wicthes on May Day Eve. On St. Martin's Day in Belgium, November 11, and Guy Fawkes Day in England, November 5th, children used to build fires and dance about them in the street. Elsewhere, especially in Nordic countries, May Day or Easter fires may be traced to procreative rites among the ancients. See *Erste Zondag*.

First Fruits: See *Weeks*.

Flag: Flag Day is also called Flag-Raising Day. On June 14, 1894, the governor of the state of New York ordered the flag to be raised on all public buildings in commemoration of Congress's adoption of the Stars and Stripes as our national flag on that date, 1777. Subsequent governors have followed his example. On August 3, 1949, President Truman signed a bill which would request the President each year to call for national observance of this day. The state of Pennsylvania observes Flag Day June 14, as a legal holiday.

Flaggans Dag: Flag Day in Sweden is a national patriotic holiday commemroating the birthday of the ruling monarch, King Gustav V. It is celebrated on June 6th.

St. Florian: St. Florian's feast day is celebrated May 4th in honor of a Roman soldier martyred in the reign of Diocletian. Perhaps because he suffered martyrdom by drowning, St. Florian was regarded as patron of fire fighters (St. Agatha's protection was invoked for fire prevention). Because of his name, St. Florian was also regarded as patron of growing things in the early spring.

Flyttedag: Flyttedag, or "the Day of Moving," is, in larger Norwegian towns, still observed in the fall of the year. On this day help is selected for the next year, and servants are free to leave their old employment and seek new if they choose to do so.

Forefathers: Forefathers' Day is also called Pilgrim's Day. Observance of the landing of Puritan pilgrims at Plymouth, Massachusetts, on December 21, 1620, originated in Protestant churches in New England during the eighteenth century. First recorded observance was in 1769.

Forrest: See *Nathan B. Forrest*.

Forty Saints: The Martyrdom of the Forty Saints of Sebastia in 320 is celebrated on the 9th of March in the Greek Orthodox Church with great veneration. In Rumania this was considered an especially important day for weather prognostication.

Foundation: The title which, before 1935, was generally given Australia Day.

Founding of the Mormon Church: The anniversary of the founding of the Church of the Latter Day Saints, on April 6, 1830, is celebrated annually at Salt Lake City, Utah, by a general conference of the church.

Founding of the Republic: October 10th, the birthday of the Chinese Republic, which began with the Wuchang Revolution in 1911, is a holiday of great political significance throughout modern China.

Fourth Month Fast: See *Tammuz*, for the Jewish fast held on the seventeenth day of Tammuz.

Fourth of July: See *Independence Day*.

St. Frances Xavier Cabrini: See Mother Cabrini.

St. Francis of Assisi: The feast day of St. Francis of Assisi, founder of the order of Friar Minor in 1226, is celebrated on the 4th of October. On September 17th the Church commemorates St. Francis' bearing of the stigmata. This is the only feasts of its kind in the Church calendar.

St. Francis Xavier: India's patron saint, who assisted Loyola in founding the Society of Jesus. His feast day is December 3rd.

St. Francois de Sales: St. Francis of Sales, Bishop of Geneva and noted Doctor of the Church was canonized in 1665. The feast day of this staunch fighter against Calvinism in France is celebrated on Jan. 29th in the Roman Catholic Church.

Franklin's Birthday: According to present reckoning Benjamin Franklin was born on January 17, 1706, and the occasion is celebrated by the Printers and Publishers Association, by the city of Philadelphia, the University of Pennsylvania and the Franklin Society.

Fraternal: The second Tuesday in October was, in 1915, established as a legal holiday in Alabama. Previous legislation had made Columbus Day a legal holiday, but in 1915 this act was repealed in favor of Fraternal Day. The occasion is now known as Columbus and Fraternal Day.

Friday: The day sacred to Friga, a Teutonic goddess analogous to the Roman Venus. Friday is a holy day to Moslems, for on a Friday, they believe, Adam was born, and on this day was taken into Paradise.

Friendship: An opportunity provided by the Greeting Card Dealers' Association for the American public to express friendly sentiments during a normally quiet business season. August 2nd was the day chosen.

Furry: The Furry Festival, an annual festival at Helsten, in Wales, celebrates on the 8th of May, the legend attached to the town's beginning. According to tradition, St. Michael intercepted the devil as he was stealing a great granite stone at the mouth of hell, and where the devil dropped the stone the town was established.

Gaense Tag: See *St. Leopold.*

Garland of Lights: See *Diwali.*

Gasparilla: The Gasparilla Carnival is an annual festival held at Tampa, Florida, on the 10th of February. In 1904 sixty young men of Tampa organized "Ye Mystic Krewe of Gasparilla" celebrating the exploits of José Gasparilla, a Spanish pirate of the eighteenth century. The capture of the city by "Ye Mystic Krewe" proved most successful.

Gautma: See *Buddha.*

Gedaliah: See *Tishri.* Third of Tishri is a minor Jewish fast day, commemorating the slaying of Gedaliah, governor of Palestine under Nebuchadnezzar.

St. Genevieve: The feast of St. Genevieve, patron saint of Paris, is celebrated January 3rd. Genevieve was said to have saved this city from the ravages of Attila the Hun. A church was built in her honor near Notre Dame, as well as another, by the Emperor Clovis, at Saint Denis.

St. Gennaro: The feast of St. Januarius, called in Italian St. Gennaro, is each year celebrated in New York as well as in Naples. The patron saint of Naples is carried in effegy through the streets on September 19th, but the festival itself generally lasts three days.

Genshi-Sai: A national holiday in Japan on January 3rd to commmorate the beginning of the first court functions of the new year.

St. George: Patron saint of England: his feast day falls on April 23rd. A native of Cappadocia in Asia Minor and soldier in the Roman army, George of Cappedocia was martyred about the year 303 in the reign of Diocletian. He is better remembered for the associations which have come to his name through the heraldic valor of the English armies than for special deeds of his own. Richard I put the country under his special protection before leaving on the Third Crusade about 1191.

In pre-Revolutionary Russia St. George's Day, on May 6th or the first day after the celebration of Easter (on or near this date), was occasion for conferring the Order of St. George's Cross and other military distinctions.

Georgia: A legal holiday in Georgia, the 12th of February commemorates John Oglethorpe's landing at Savannah in 1733, and the first settlement of what became the state of Georgia.

German Settlement: Anniversary of the first permanent German settlement in America at Germantown, Pennsylvania, has frequently been observed on October 6th, by descendants of German settlers in this country.

Gettysburg: July 1st celebrations and informal observances commemorate the battle between the Armies of the Potomac and of Northern Virginia which was to check the northern advance of Lee's army and turn the tide of the Civil War.

Giarwin Sharif: Literally, "blessed eleventh," a Moslem holiday set aside for prayers. Giarwin Sharif falls on the eleventh day of the month of Rabiussani, and is the saint day of Hazrat Ghulam Zadir Jilani, a great saint of Islam.

Girl Scout: The first meeting of a group of girls calling themselves the Girl Guides was held on March 12, 1912, at the home of Mrs. Juliette Low, of Savannah, Georgia. Through

Mrs. Low's acquaintance with Sir Robert Baden-Powell, founder of the Boy Scout movement, the organization developed along similar lines and in 1915 was incorporated as the Girl Scouts of America.

Glorification du Fondateur: See *Haitian Independence.*

Gokulstami: See *Krishna.*

Good Friday: The day of the Passion has been observed as a principal festival of the Christian Church from earliest times. The story of the convening of the court which tried Jesus is best recounted in the Gospel of Luke (22), of his examination by Pilate in John (18), of the final sentence and crucifixion at Golgotha, a place near Jerusalem (John 19-20, Luke 23). The origin of the term is obscured, however, in the irony of the term or the breakdown in pronunciation of "God's Friday." The solemnity of the occasion has, from the first, precluded legal and public functions in all Christian states and has been celebrated by the greatest musical and artistic creations of Christian times.

Grange: During the Rogation Days (Monday, Tuesday and Wednesday before Ascension Day) the ancient English custom of perambulating the parish was accompanied by feasting and merrymaking. Parts of the traditional festivities were curtailed under Elizabeth I, but traces of the custom remain in rural England. The term is derived from the Anglo Saxon *"gangen,"* meaning "to go."

Great Thursday: See *Maundy Thursday.* The day preceding Good Friday is an especially important occasion in the Greek Orthodox Church. The highest dignitary washes the feet of his inferiors in memory of Christ's action at the Last Supper.

Greece: Greek independence from Turkish rule was established in 1812; the date is usually celebrated on the Sunday nearest March 25th.

St. Gregory: Pope Gregory I is considered one of the four great Latin Fathers of the Church. His feast day falls on March 12th. Gregory was instrumental in perfecting both the ritual and music of the Roman Catholic Church and was active in reviving Christianity among the Saxon tribes on the

British Isles. St. Gregory Nazianzen, Bishop and Doctor of the Church is remembered on May 9th.

Grito: *Grito de Baire* (*de Yara*), the yell which marked the triumph of Cuba's thirty-year struggle for independence from Spanish rule. See *Mexico.*

Groundhog: (See *Candlemas.*) A traditional belief, still popular in the United States, claims that six more weeks of winter weather are forthcoming if, on the 2nd of February, the ground hog can see his own shadow.

Grover Cleveland: Grover Cleveland's birthday, March 18th, was, at one time, the occasion for anniversary celebrations in his honor given by the National Democratic party and public-minded citizens of New York.

Guadalupe: The feast of the Virgin of Guadalupe falls on December 12th. *Nuestra Señora de Guadalupe* is a great fiesta among the devout of Mexico and in southwestern United States. Her miraculous appearance to Juan Diego, a convert hurrying to Mass near Mexico City on this day in 1531, is observed with pilgrimages to her church, outside Mexico City. In the Mexican War for Independence, Our Lady of Guadalupe was made the patron saint of the revolutionary army and therefore became the patroness of Mexico.

Guatamelan Independence: September 15th marks the anniversary of Gutemala's independence from Spain.

Guddhi Padava: See *Dhvajoropana.*

Gule of August: See *Lammas.*

Guru Nanak: The birthday of their founder is the most important holiday of the Sikhs. Pilgrims from districts of Pakistan and India visit the birthplace of the Guru and other holy places where he spent the last years of his life. (See *Sikh Holidays.*)

Gustavus Adolphus: *Gustav Adolfsdagen* on November 6th commemorates the Battle of Lutzen of 1632. It is a Swedish national holiday. On this day Sweden's great national hero, Gustavus Adolphus, was killed.

Gutenberg: While the exact date of Johannes Gutenberg's birth is not known, February 23rd has become sufficiently well established to mark the occasion of anniversaries celebrating the invention of the printing press, or emphasizing the value of learning and reading in general.

Guy Fawkes: Guy Fawkes's plot to blow up the Houses of Parliament in 1605 was part of a much larger struggle between Catholicism and Protestantism in England. But the custom of lighting bonfires and carrying Guy Fawkes in effigy on the 5th of November survives, in England, to this day.

Hadj: Moslem pilgrimages to Mecca are composed of three main rituals: the sevenfold circumambulation of the Kaaba, the great central edifice at Mecca, the Lesser sevenfold pilgrimage between Safa and Marwa in commemoration of Hagar's search for water, and the Greater Pilgrimage to the Mount of Mercy in the plain of Ararat.

Haitian Independence: The legal holiday of the *Glorification du Fondateur at des Héros de l'Indépendence* (of Haiti) is celebrated to the glory of the founders and heroes of Haitian independence, secured in 1927. On this occasion wreathes are placed at the tomb of Emperor Dessalines and President Pétion.

Halifax Resolutions of Independence: These resolutions, adopted by North Carolina on April 12, 1776, played an important part in the acceptance of the Declaration of Independence. The occasion is remembered by a holiday in North Carolina on the anniversary of this date.

Halloween: October 31st, the eve of All Saints' Day, All Hallow's Eve. This day has accumulated many traditions reaching back to the time of the Druids in England and of the Roman festival to Pomona, goddess of the harvest. The cat was sacred to the Druids, who on this night lit fires honoring the festival of the sun god. Harvest symbols, such as pumpkins, stem from Roman traditions. There is some suggestion that All Saints' Day was itself instituted to divert attention from lingering pagan traditions. See *All Saints' Day*.

Han Lu: The traditional Chinese festival of Han Lu, or Dew Grows Cold, marks the passing of summer. At Han Lu summer is treated as a friend who must go on a long trip.

Han Shih: Immediately preceding the Pure and Bright Festival of spring (Ch'ing Ming) comes the traditional Chi-

nese observance of the Han Shih or Cold Food days. During
these three days of April, fires are permitted to go out and
food is eaten cold, if at all. (See *Ch'ing Ming.*)

Handsel Monday: The Scotch counterpart of the English
Boxing Day falls on the first Monday of the new year. The
term derives from the Old English "earnest money" and, especially in Scotland, indicated the first money received at mar-
ket. Handsels or presents of money thus were given as tokens
of good will for the ensuing new year.

St. Hans: St. John's (Midsummer Eve) in Norway, celebrated, in the northern regions, with smudge fires, since on
this night the sun still is shining, for it is the longest night of
the year.

Hanukkah: The Jewish Feast of Lights, also called Feast
of Dedication. Hanukkah begins the twenty-fifth day of Kislev, the ninth sacred month of the Jewish calendar, and lasts
eight days. Though not mentioned in the Bible, the story of
Judah the Maccabee's victory over the Syrian forces and their
rededication of the Temple is told in the First and Second
Books of the Maccabees, in the Apocrypha. The theme of national victory has, since Roman times, been somwhat subordi-
nated to the spiritual symbol of relighting the Temple can-
delabrum, which lights symbolize the eternal light shining
through the spirit of the Jewish people.

Harvest: The name is derived from the Anglo-Saxon "haer-
fest," but the principle of celebrating the ingathering of the
crops is as old as man and common to all people. It is celebrated in the Jewish Feast of the Tabernacles, was observed
by the Romans in honor of Ceres and by Chinese in honor
of the Moon (Chung-Ch'iu). Harvest ceremonies commonly
are associated with the religion of the country in which they
are observed; special thanksgiving is made or, as in Armenia
where the Blessing of the Grapes falls on Assumption Day, the
occasion is celebrated on a religious holiday.

Hawaiian Song: The second Sunday in May winning songs
of a three-months contest are given public performance in
Honolulu.

Hegira: Islam begins its calendar from the Year of the

Flight, Anno Hegira, July 16, 622, when Mohammed fled from Mecca to Medina (then Yathrib). See *Muharram*.

Hidalgo: One of the greatest of Mexican holidays begins on September 15th. On that day in 1810 Father Miguel Hidalgo y Costilla first cried out for independence. Mexican Independence Day begins today with the famous shout to freedom, the *"grito."*

High Places: For the Chinese festival of High Places, see *Ch'ung Yang*. This festival corresponds to the Japanese festival of Kite-Flying Day.

St. Hilary: Since the Church of England celebrates St. Hilary's day on the 13th of January, the Hilary term begins at Cambridge on this date but on the 14th at Oxford. St. Hilary, Doctor and one of the Fathers of the Latin Church, was elected Bishop of Poitiers in 354.

Hillula: The *hillula* of Rabbi Simeon ben Yohai, celebrating the death of the "father of Jewish mysticism" is celebrated in Palestine on Lag b'Omer. Bonfires, singing and dancing characterizes the mystic "wedding" of all levels of existence which were united in the soul of the Rabbi. See *Lag B'Omer*.

Hina-no-Sekku: The popular Festival of Dolls or Girls' Doll Festival in Japan, also known as the Peach Festival. Hina-No-Sekku especially honors girls as Tango-no-Sekku, the Feast of Banners, honors boys. It falls at the time of the flowering of the peach trees and is celebrated on March 3rd.

Hindu Holidays: While a few holidays peculiar to the Hindu religion are mentioned in this book, it is difficult for the Western world to follow Hindu fete days. Most of these are derived from the earliest days, called the Vedic Age, when nearly every object and element was personified and deified. These gods have been reincarnated, have intermarried and multiplied. Important holidays are assigned to the events which pertain to the three great gods, Brahma the Creator, Vishnu the Preserver, and Siva the Destroyer. And while all gods are manifestations of the One God, each has distinct rituals and separate functions and, depending on the locality, may have a number of names. Further, there are many sects of Hinduism, and the sacred books are not familiar to Western readers. Perhaps simplest to follow is the matter of new year celebrations celebrating the commencement of each season. These occur at Dhvajoropana (or Guddhi Padva), Makara Sankranti, Diwali, and Ratha Yathra, the four seasons of spring, winter, autumn and summer respectively.

The complexity of Hindu calends is attested by the regional divergence in the celebration of New Year's Day. The Gujeratis of Western India have traditionally begun the new year with the Diwali celebrations the third week in October. The Telegus of Central India have observed New Year's Day on April 1st, the Sikhs (North India) and the Amils (South India) on April 13th. See *Indian Calendar*.

Hogmenay: (also Hogomenay) New Year's Day and New Year's Eve revels were occasionally known, in the north of England and in Scotland, as Hogmenay. Various customs are ascribed to the day, which appears to have a pre-Christian origin.

Hol Ha-Moed: The five day interval betwen the first two and the last two days of Succoth, the Jewish Feast of the Tabernacles, is known as *Hol ha-Moed*. This intervening time, analagous to the week days of Holy Week before Easter, are observed by the Orthodox Jews as semi-holidays.

Holi: The Fire Festival, great spring festival in India, Holi is a great carnival occasion, especially in northern India. It is characterized by the splashing of colored water, the use of color, and building of bonfires. It is preceded by Basanta and falls generally in March, on the fifteenth day of the month of Phalguna. In Bengal called Doljatra Swing Festival.

Holmenkollen: The international ski meet and winter sports event in Norway is held at Holmenkollen, Oslo, Norway, the last of February. It reaches its climax on Holmenkollen Day, the first wek in March, when the Royal Family and King watch the ski-jumping competitions.

Holy Cross: See Exaltation of the Cross and Finding of the Cross.

Holy Family: A day of obligation in the Western Church, commemorating the domestic life of Jesus, the Virgin Mary, and Joseph, on the second Sunday of January.

Holy Innocents: Before the Reformation the Christian Church celebrated the festival of Holy Innocents' Day, also called Childermas and Innocents' Day, with much pageantry on Dec. 28th. It commemorated Herod's slaughter of male children in Bethlehem shortly after the birth of Christ.

Holy Name: The feast of the Holy Name of Jesus, originally a celebration of the Franciscan Order alone, was extended to the entire Church in 1721 by Pope Innocent XIII. It commemorates the naming of Jesus at the time of his circumcision. (See also *Circumcision.*) It is celebrated January 2nd unless the 3rd, 4th, or 5th is a Sunday, in which case the later date takes precedence.

Holy Name: The feast of the Holy Name, a Roman Catholic feast day celebrated on the second Sunday after Epiphany. The occasion for the first feast, in 1274, appears to have arisen out of political difficulties with the Albigensians, but a parade undertaken in honor of the Holy Name in 1432 is reputed to have had salutary effects in relieving the oft-plague-ridden Lisbon, Portugal.

Holy Rood: See *Exaltation of the Cross.*

Holy Saturday: The Saturday preceding Easter Sunday, now called, in the Roman Catholic Church, the Vigil of Easter.

Holy Thursday: The Thursday of Holy Week is properly called Holy Thursday, though Ascension Day is also called by this name. The liturgy of the Roman Catholic Church commemorates, on Holy Thursday, the institution of the Holy Eucharist, offering of the first Mass, ordination of the apostles as priests, the agony of Christ in the Garden of Gethsemane, and the beginning of the Passion.

Holy Week: The last week of Lent, beginning with Palm Sunday, preceding Easter.

Hospital: Since 1920, the centenary of the birth of Florence Nightingale, May 12th, National Hospital Day has been set aside to mark the advances made in care and prevention of diseases.

Huey P. Long: By the governor's proclamation, August 30th was made a legal holiday in Louisiana in honor of former Governor Huey Long.

Huguenot: April 13th, the anniversary of the important Edict of Nantes (1598) by which the citizens of Nantes were given religious liberty. This day was especially a Protestant holiday in France and for descendants of Huguenot refugees who settled in the new world.

Hukilau: A monthly festival (except in December) held in Polynesian communities, now principally on the islands of Oahu and Hawaii. The entire community joined in pulling in an enormous fishing seine which was fringed with leaves and laid in a semicircle in the bay. The Hukilau (literally, "to pull the leaves") is generally held on the last Saturday of the month.

Hozhanna Rabba: The seventh day of the Jewish Feast of Tabernacles is marked by a special ceremony which originally symbolized a special plea for an abundance of water. The day later came to be associated with the last of the days of judgment which begin with *Rosh Ha-Shanah.*

Hungary: Hungary's first attempt at independence, under the direction of Louis Kossuth in 1848, is observed by Free Hungarians on March 15th. See also Petöfi.

Husain's Martyrdom: Each year many of Islam re-enact the drama of the death and martyrdom of Halrat Imam Husain, grandson of the Prophet. Husain fell in battle at Kerbela, near Bagdad, on the 10th of Muharram, 61 A.H. (October 9, 680 A.D.). See *Muharram.*

Huss: John Huss, Bohemian religious martyr, was burned at the stake on July 6, 1415. This occasion was, before the last world war, a Czech national holiday.

Hussein I: On November 14th Jordanians celebrate the birthday of their King, H. M. Hussein I, born in 1935, as a national holiday.

I Am An American Day: Set aside in 1940 for observance on the third Sunday in May, the date has, since this time, occasioned many patriotic celebrations in the United States.

'Id Al-Adha: Islam's three-day festival of sacrifice celebrated the 9th through 12th days of Thi Alhijjah, the twelfth Moslem month, in honor of Abraham's faith in God in being willing to sacrifice his son Ishmael. A voice from heaven intervened and stayed the father's hand. According to Moslem tradition, Jews are descendants of Abraham's son Isaac, while descendants of Ishmael became Arabs. 'Id al-Adha is also a day of memorial to the dead. By the Gregorian calendar it is celebrated in June or July.

'Id Al-Fitr: One of the five tenets of Islam is observance of the fast of Ramadan (which see); 'Id al-Fitr marks th end of this fast month with a three-day celebration beginning the first day of Shawwal, the tenth lunar month of the Moslem calendar. It is an especially festive occasion with great fairs and festivity. By the Gregorian calendar 'Id al-Fitr falls in April or May.

'Id Al-Jami 'A Al-Arabiyyah: On March 22nd the anniversary of the Arab League Pact of 1945 is celebrated annually in Jordan and other member countries.

'Id Al-Milad An-Nabi: The Birthday of the Prophet, celebrated by the faithful of Islam for a period of nine days, generally on the anniversary of his death in the month of Abib. A day of great rejoicing among followers of the Prophet.

'Id El-Ghastas: In the Coptic Church, Epiphany, celebrated in the lunar Moslem month of Kihak.

'Id El-Milad: In the Coptic Church, Christmas, celebrated on the date comparable to December 25th on the Gregorian calendar.

'Id El-Salib: In the Coptic Church, the Festival of the Cross (Palm Sunday), celebrated in the lunar Moslem month of Tut.

Idaho Pioneer: Commemoration of the founding of the first settlement in Idaho, at Franklin, on January 15, 1860. See *Pioneer*.

Idris Assanusi I: The anniversary of King Idris Assanusi I, born March 12, 1890, is a national holiday in Libya.

St. Ignatius: July 3rd is the feast day of St. Ignatius of Loyola who founded the order of the Society of Jesus in 1534. Loyola was canonized by Gregory XV in 1622. St. Ignatius of

Antioch, Bishop and martyr remembered for his early theological writings, is also important in Roman Catholic martyrology. His feast day, February 1st, is a day of total abstinence.

Immaculate Conception: The feast of the Immaculate Conception is celebrated throughout the Western and Eastern Church. It appears to have been introduced into the West by way of Naples about the ninth century, originating in Constantinople (as the Syllepsis of the Mother of God), and was generally celebrated in Sicily and lower Italy as the Conception of St. Anne, meaning that St. Anne conceived Mary, mother of Christ. The belief that Mary was without original sin had, however, a much earlier origin. The feast day, officially recognized by the Church in 1477 and established on December 8th as a holy day of obligation by Pope Clement XI in 1721, was not defined until 1854. This day has been observed as a public holiday in Spain since the seventeenth century.

Immaculate Heart of Mary: A feast of the Roman Catholic Church commemorating the consecration of the world to her Immaculate Heart by Pope Pius XII in 1942, on August 22nd.

Inauguration: From Washington's inauguration in 1789, the date for this occasion had been established as March 4th. But in 1933 Congress changed the date to January 20th, the first celebration occurring in 1937 according to the Twentieth Amendment to the Constitution. Inauguration Day is a legal holiday in the District of Columbia and Baton Rouge, Louisiana, only.

Independence: The national U.S. holiday celebrating the signing of the Declaration of Independence by members of the Continental Congress, at the State House in Philadelphia. While all colonies had actually acted upon the measures then under consideration and independence had been declared on July 2nd, Jefferson's document was not acted upon until the fourth of July. General Washington ordered the first celebration of the signing to be held July 9, 1776, and an unofficial celebration had been held the preceding night at Philadelphia. The next year the army observed the occasion with an extra gill of rum ordered for every soldier at Morristown, and in 1779 the Commander-in-Chief ordered a general pardon for all prisoners-of-war under sentence of death, to celebrate the Fourth.

Independence Day is, for most countries, a special patriotic holiday.

Indian Calendar: On March 22, 1957, the government of India presented an official calendar which established that date as Chaitra 1, 1879, Saka Era. This calendar takes its name from the dynasty in control in Northern India in the year 78 A.D., when the first scientifically prepared calendar was introduced. March 22nd is the day following the Vernal Equinox. The new calendar is not mandatory, though it will regulate government business.

The committee appointed to study the problem reported that not less than thirty different calendars were in use in various parts of India in the year 1955. The first calendar used in India, employed by the Vedic Aryans (until about 1350 B.C.), was followed by the Vedang Jyotish period (1350 B.C. to 400 A.D.). Knowledge of the Vedic calendar is derived from a study of the hymns of the Rig Veda. The Vedang Jyotish calendar, which disappeared about 400 A.D., was a lunar calendar based on a Yug of fifty-two lunar months and 60 solar months, representing a period of about five years. The best known succeeding system, emerging about 550 A.D., was the Siddhanta Jyotish calendar. It divided the year into twelve lunar months but permitted an error of twenty-four minutes each tropical year, with the result that the fixed month of Chaitra, which marked the commencement of the new year immediately after the vernal equinox, began twenty-three days late. It is this error which the new calendar seeks to correct.

With the Islamic domination of India in 1200 A.D., the Siddhanta Jyotish calendar was abandoned except for isolated communities. The lunar Hijra calendar was used for all administrative purposes until, in 1584, the Emperor Akbar introduced a new calendar called the Tarikh Illahi. In 1757 the British, who thereafter took over the civil administration of the country, regulated affairs by the Gregorian calendar.

Indian Child: See *Juarez*.

Indiana: Indiana's admission into the Union on December 11, 1816, is usually celebrated as a holiday in that state.

Indonesia: Proclamation of Indonesian independence was made August 17, 1945, by President Sukarno.

Ingathering: See *Tabernacles*.

Innocents: See *Holy Innocents*.

Inocentes: In Mexico such April Fool's Day pranks as are common to European countries and North America are reserved for the *Dia de los Inocentes,* on the 28th of December. In the British Isles and parts of Europe Holy Innocents' Day had also occasioned family frolic.

Intertribal Indian Ceremonial: The intertribal ceremonial at Gallup, New Mexico, held each year the last three days of August, has, in recent years, grown in importance and pretentiousness. Both Pueblo and Plains Indian nations participate, though originally the Hopi, Navajo and Zuni peoples were the principals.

Invention of the Cross: May 3rd at one time commemorated the discovery, by the Empress Helena, mother of Constantine the Great, of the Holy Cross on which Christ had been crucified. The cross was probably the greatest of many relics popular during the Middle Ages. Entrusted to the Bishop of Jerusalem until the conquest of 614, at which time it was removed to Persia, the cross, like many sacred relics of the period, was greatly venerated by faithful pilgrims. This feast day is also known as the Finding of the Holy Cross.

St. Isidore: St. Isidore the Ploughman is patron saint of Madrid and of farmers. In Spain especially he is honored by fiestas, the greatest of which is held in Madrid on his feast day, May 10th. St. Isidore of Seville, Bishop and Doctor of the Church (560-630) is remembered on April 4th for his learned counsel and reverent life.

Jackson: See *Stonewall Jackson*.

Jackson: Otherwise known as "Old Hickory Day" in commemoration of the anniversary of the Battle of New Orleans which General Andrew Jackson won on Jan. 8, 1815. This day is a legal holiday in Louisiana.

Jagannath: See *Procession of the Chariots.*

St. James: One of the apostles of Jesus, of the two Jameses called the "Greater" because he was, with Peter, Andrew and John, one of the four leaders of the twelve disciples. According to legend, James aided the Spaniards against the Saracens, and his day, July 25th, is one of the greatest holidays in Spain. Called the Apostle of Spain. His shrine at Compostella is honored by many pilgrimages. St. James the Less was also an Apostle, first Bishop of Jerusalem and martyred there about 62 A.D. He was a cousin of Christ, the author of an epistle. His feast day is celebrated by the Catholic Church on May 11th.

Jammashtami: The Hindu festival in honor of the birth of the Lord Krishna. Actually the Jammashtami may refer to a number of festivals devoted to Vishnu, embodiment of the creative spirit. The most important of these are associated with his eighth incarnation as Lord Krishna, whose birth is celebrated in the summer as a great Hindu holiday. See *Krishna.*

St. Januarius: See *St. Gennaro.*

Jefferson: April 13th, Thomas Jefferson's Birthday is celebrated in Alabama, Missouri, Oklahoma and Virginia, and by the Democratic party as the occasion of its annual banquet.

Jefferson Davis: June 3rd has been a legal holiday in Florida since 1892, and in eight other Southern states, in honor of the anniversary of the birth of the President of the Confederacy. Jefferson Davis was born in 1808; he was inaugurated President of the Seceding States on February 22, 1862, and died on December 6, 1889.

St. Jerome: The 30th of September is observed by all branches of the Western Catholic Church in honor of the scholarship of St. Jerome, his missionary work, and the monasteries he founded. St. Jerome, one of the four great Fathers of the Latin Church, translated the Bible into Latin. This edition is known as the Vulgate.

Jewish New Year: See *Blowing of the Trumpet.*

St. Joachim: The feast day of St. Joachim, father of the Blessed Virgin Mary, is celebrated August 16th. It is a day of total abstinence in the Roman Catholic Church.

Joan of Arc: Fête de Jeanne d'Arc (May 30th) is a festival day in France, especially at Rouen and Orléans, in honor of the Maid, whose martyrdom on May 30, 1431, has been celebrated by the Church since 1909.

John The Baptist: Four church festivals are associated with St. John the Baptist, beheaded by Herod. The first of these festivals, the anniversary of his nativity, has been assigned to June 24th (January 7th in the Greek Orthodox Church). During the Middle Ages this feast day was first in importance of saint days. On August 29th the anniversary of the Beheading of John the Baptist (see *Beheading Day*) is observed. Much more recently adopted from the Oriental (Coptic) Church is the celebration of his baptism of the Lord, observed on January 13th in the Latin Church (January 6th in the Greek Orthodox Church). The Oriental Church also observes St. John's Conception.

St. John the Baptist is patron saint of Puerto Rico, of shepherds, tailors and masons.

St. John Chrysostom: The feast of St. John Chrysostom, Bishop of Constantinople, is observed in the Western Church on January 27th, in the Eastern on the 30th of January (Feast of the Three Hierarchs: Basil the Great, Gregory the Theologian and John Chrysostom). A great preacher and writer of the Christian Church, he was born in Antioch about 345. For a time he was known, because of his good works, as John the Almoner, but later he came to be called Chrysostom, the "golden-mouthed" for the beauty and excellence of his words.

St. John's Eve: While St. John's Day was not established on June 24th in order to Christianize pagan solstice celebrations, as some have suspected, the later adoption of the Gregorian calendar established a coincidence between St. John's Eve and the summer solstice, on June 23rd. The practice of lighting fires on this occasion (originally *niedfyr* or "need fires") remains throughout Europe, Russia and the British

Isles. In Finland these are called *Juhannusaatto*, in Burgundy and Brittany *Feux de la Saint Jean*, in Austria *Johannesfeier*, throughout Latvia *Janu Vakars*, and are built on hilltops. In Spain bonfires (*fogatas*) are lit in the streets, and in other parts of Europe (notably France) people light torches or with a blessed candle ignite straw attached to wagon wheels which are rolled down the hills.

St. John The Evangelist: The feast of St. John the Evangelist, the son of Zebedee and "beloved disciple" of Christ is celebrated December 27th. John wrote the fourth Gospels and three epistles, and the Apocalypse. Though banished from the Roman Empire to the isle of Patmos, he did not suffer martyrdom. He is purported to have died in the year 101.

Jordan: Jordanian independence is celebrated on May 25th in honor of the inception of the Kingdom of Jordan, in 1946.

St. Joseph: The feast day of Joseph, Jesus's foster-father, is especially popular among the Italian people as patron of the Church and workmen. It is celebrated on March 19th and May 1st. The latter feast is dedicated to St. Joseph the Workman.

Juarez: Birthday of Benito Juárez is a national holiday in Mexico. The great Mexican patriot and defender of freedom was born on March 21, 1806. It was he who led the first battles against feudalism and became first President of the Republic in 1861. This same year Napoleon III attempted to establish Maximilian as Emperor of Mexico. Juárez's defense of the nation's sovereignty was eventually successful. Since Juárez was Indian, his day is also known as the Day of the Indian Child.

Judas: See *Saturday of Glory*; also *Fires*.

Jude: Also called Thaddeus, who was, according to tradition, brother of James the Less. His feast day is celebrated on October 28th in the Western Church, June 19th in the Eastern.

Judgment: For the Jewish feast of the Day of Judgment see *Blowing of the Trumpet*.

Jumat-Ul-Wida: Literally, the "Friday of leavetaking," celebrated the last Friday of the month of Ramadan (which see).

In Islamic countries, a public holiday. At midday prayer on this Friday (Moslems are required to pray five times each day) there are special forms for the close of Ramadan.

Kagami-Biraki: The Japanese ceremony of cutting and eating pounded rice cakes called Mochi especially prepared for the New Year, celebrated the 11th of January.

Kalevala: February 28th is a Finnish national holiday honoring Elias Lönnrot who gathered together Finnish ballads and poems and discovered the great national epic *Kalevala*.

Kallemooi: A Whitsun Eve tradition on the islands of the north coast of Holland similar to that of the English maypole ceremonies on May Day.

Kamahameha: In Hawaii and among the Polynesian peoples, a celebration beginning June 11th, usually lasting several days, in honor of Kamehameha the Great, first King and "Napoleon of the Pacific." Kamehameha and his descendants ruled the islands for a century before Hawaii was annexed to the United States.

Kanname-Sai: Japan celebrates two harvest festivals. The first, Kanname-Sai, is a national fete day honoring the new grain. Offerings are made by the Emperor to his imperial ancestors and by his subjects to theirs. At the second ceremony, Niiname-Sai, the Emperor himself partakes of the new grain. Kanname-Sai is held October 17th.

Kansas: The anniversary of Kansas' admission into the Union, approved on January 29, 1861, has become a popular occasion for dinners and celebrations by the Republican party in that state.

Kentucky Derby: Since May 17, 1875, this has undoubtedly been the greatest horse-racing event in this country. It is now held on May 5th.

Khao Phansa: July 25th, marks the beginning of Buddhist Lent which more or less corresponds with the rainy season. The period of Lent starts on the 1st of the waning of the eighth month and continues till the twelfth month (of the lunar calendar).

Khordadsal: The birthday of Lord Zoroaster. See *Zarathustra*.

Kigensetsu: February 11th, the anniversary of one of Japan's four great emperors, Jimmu Tenno, in 660 B.C., is a traditional holiday. Special services are conducted at the court.

Killing of the Pigs: An Estonian and Magyar tradition popular among rural families in Esthonia and Hungary, of making a great feast, some time in September, at which time the pigs were slaughtered and the meat prepared for the winter. In Rumania the family pig, especially fattened for the holidays, is killed on St. Ignatius's feast day.

Kings: For the Feast of the Kings, as it sometimes is called, see the *Tabernacles*.

Kitchen God: See *Tsao Chün*.

Kite-Flying Day: The Chinese holiday of Ch'ung Yang Chieh is a special day for men and boys; it is celebrated the ninth day of the Ninth Month.

Kourban Bairam: Preferred Turkish term for Mohemmedan Feast of Sacrifice, 'Id al-Adha (which see).

Krishna: The Hindu god Vishnu, the Preserver, took many forms to save the world and its people. In his eighth incarnation he appeared as Krishna, whose birthday (Janmashtami or Gokulstami) is celebrated by Hindus with special mantras, foods and celebrations. See *Hindu Holidays*.

Kruger Day: October 10th, Kruger Day, is a state holiday in the Union of South Africa in memory of President Paul Kruger and other heroes of South Africa. Stephanus Johannes Paulus Kruger was born on this day, 1825, of Huguenot ancestry, and represented Boer interests through his three terms as President of the Transvaal.

Kuhio: March 26th, a legal holiday in the Territory of Hawaii, to honor the birthday anniversay of Prince Kuhio, first delegate to Congress from Hawaii.

Kyriake: "The Day of the Lord," by which name Sunday is known in the Greek Orthodox Church, though in the liturgy the term "Resurrection" (Anastasis) is also used.

Labor: In 1894 Congress passed a law making legal the observance of Labor Day as a public holiday to be celebrated the first Monday in September, the day "celebrated and known as Labor's Holiday." Actually, Congressional action merely recognized the importance of the date; individual states must act upon public holidays in their own right. The first Labor Day was celebrated in New York in 1882 upon the suggestion of Peter J. McGuire of the Knights of Labor. Labor Day is now observed in all states and territories except Alabama, but it is not generally a bank holiday.

Lady: See *Annunciation*. Until 1752 this date, March 25th, was the beginning of the legal year in England.

Lady Godiva: An annual procession in Coventry, England, on August 2nd still celebrates this tradesman's holiday. The occasion relates to the sacrifice imposed on Lady Godiva that she ride through the streets with only her hair to hide her nakedness in return for granting her wish that Coventry should have its freedom.

Lag B'omer: On the thirty-third day of the "omer," a seven-week lenten period in the Jewish religious calendar, restrictions are suddenly relaxed, festivities are in order, such as are equivalent to May Day customs. Lag b'Omer falls on the 18th of Iyar and so occurs near the first of May, Gregorian calendar. In Palestine the *hillula* of Rabbi Simeon ben Yohai is observed on this date.

Lammas: Originally one of the great pagan festivals in Britain, Lammas Day derives its name from "half-mass," offering of a small loaf of bread given the church during the early stages of Christianity in Britain as the usual feast-day contribution. The early name, Gule of August ("gwyl" means "festival"), signifies the grain-harvest nature of the original celebration. The church on this day, August 1st, celebrates the festival of St. Peter's miraculous deliverance from prison.

Landing: In Wisconsin Landing Day is the preferred name for Columbus Day, October 12th.

Lanterns: For the Chinese Feast of Lanterns, see Teng Chieh; the Japanese Feast of Lanterns is called O-Bon.

Last Supper: See *Eucharist*.

Laundresses: Mid-Lent or the fourth Sunday of Lent is celebrated in parts of Paris with the traditional Festival of

the Blanchisseuses, a popular tradition during which the
queen of each district is chosen to reign during Mi-Carême.

Lazarus Saturday: In the Russian and Greek Orthodox
Church as in the Eastern (Coptic) Church, the Saturday before Palm (or Willow) Sunday was devoted to Lazarus' memory. On this day willows were gathered for the following day.
The Latin Church does not associate this day with Lazarus'
rising.

Lazybones: See *Luilak*, the Saturday before Whitsunday,
as observed in the Netherlands.

Leap Year: A year whose number is exactly divisible by
four. By the astronomers who established the Julian calendar
our year should contain 365 days and 6 hours. Each four
years these supernumerary hours are tacked together to make
an extra day which, at the end of February, jumps one day
of the week. By custom and law in Scotland, England and
France women might on this day choose whatever single
men they wished to be their husbands, the latter being obliged
to forfeit a sum of money, marry the lady, or prove his in-
tentions of marrying another.

Lee: The birthday of Robert E. Lee is a legal and public
holiday in a number of states, among them Alabama, Arkansas
and Florida. Lee was born on January 19, 1807.

Lee-Jackson: The state of Virginia honors both Andrew
Jackson and Robert E. Lee on the 23rd of February.

Legal Holiday: A holiday assumes special importance in
relation to the validity of legal papers drawn up on such
dates or contracts due on holidays. In the United States holidays are fixed by state or territorial legislation; contracts entered into on a legal holiday are, in most states, valid, but
debts are payable on the first business day after a holiday.
Sundays are, in all states, holidays, and Saturdays are, in most
states, half-holidays by law.

Lei: May Day in Hawaii is dedicated to the lei, symbol of
the hospitality of the Islands. Lei Day was first held in 1928
with pageants and appropriate celebrations.

Lent: The greatest period of fasting in the Christian
Church, originally lasting forty hours; since the Middle Ages

Lent continues for forty week days and six Sundays. Lent begins forty week days before Easter, on Ash Wednesday. It is a period of preparation for Holy Week and commences, in theological relevance, with Jesus' temptation. The last seven days of Lent are called Holy Week.

St. Leonard: In some parts of Bavaria the Leonhardritt or festival of what is known as Leonard's Ride still is traditional. On this occasion the peasants decorate their wagons and horses and ride to church in procession. Some bring their cattle to the church to be blessed. St. Leonard of Port Maurice, Confessor, whose feast day is May 26th, is noted for having spread the devotion known as Stations of the Cross.

St. Leopold: Celebration of Austria's patron saint on November 15th marks the opening of the new wine season. Many make the pilgrimage to the saint's shrine at Klosterneuburg, where a twelve-thousand-gallon wine cask plays an important part in the festivites. St. Leopold's Day also called Gaense Tag for the traditional evening meal of roast goose.

Lesser Bairam: A Mohammedan feast lasting three days. This feast follows the thirty-day fast of the month of Ramadan.

Leyden: *Leiden Ontzet* is the anniversary of the lifting of the Seige of Leyden, celebrated on October 3rd throughout the Netherlands. The seige, laid down by the Spaniards in 1573-4, was broken by the Prince of Orange, who opened the dikes and flooded the countryside.

Liberation: The anniversary of the liberation of a country has, in this day, a number of meanings. Dominating governments are wont to celebrate the conquest of the countries they have just overcome. But it is also an occasion for patriotic rejoicing and frequently associated with the anniversary of national independence. Italy celebrates the anniversary of her liberation by Allied forces on April 25, 1945, as a national legal holiday.

Liberator: See *Simon Bolivar*, called the Great Liberator.

Li Chum: "Spring Is Here" Day was a holiday of considerable importance in traditional China. On this occasion the ground was officially turned for the first time in the spring, and five colored water buffalo, symbols of long life and prosperity, were carried in effigy in a procession. Li Chum takes place in the early part of the first, or Holiday Moon, month or in the latter part of the twelfth, the Bitter Moon, month.

Life-Giving Fountain: On the Friday following Easter the Greek Orthodox Church celebrates the miracle of the discovery of the Life-Giving Fountain. Leo, Emperor of Constantinople, was directed to it by a miracle, and later he built a church on the spot.

Light: See *Epiphany* and *Hanukkah.*

Lincoln: Illinois was the first state to make February 12th a legal holiday, in 1892. But the first formal celebration of Lincoln's birth was held somewhat earlier, in Washington, D.C., in 1866, the year following his death, when both Houses convened to hear a speech in the late President's honor. The date is now annually celebrated in twenty-seven states.

Little Bairam: The period of feasting which follows *Ramadan,* which see.

Long: See *Huey P. Long.*

Long Friday: A Saxon variation of Good Friday used principally in Nordic countries.

Lord Mayor: November 9th. Elected at Michaelmas, the Lord Mayor of London begins his duties with a procession through the city to the Guild Hall and, later, to Westminster.

Lots: For the Feast of Lots, see *Purim.*

Low Sunday: A term occasionally applied to the first Sunday after Easter, presumably because Easter itself is the highest point of the Christian calendar.

Loyola: See *St. Ignatius Loyola.*

St. Lucy: December 13th is the feast day of St. Lucia of Syracuse, martyred, in the days of Diocletian, 304 A.D. In Sweden the day marked the end of all harvesting, weaving and spinning for the year. St. Lucy's day begins the second Ember Week marking the vernum period of special prayers and fasting in the Roman Catholic Church.

Luilak: The Dutch Luilak or "Lazybones' Day" falls on the eve and night of the Saturday before Whitsunday. At this time the children may demand sweets at any time of the night;

anyone who refuses to answer to their importuning would be a "luilak" the rest of the year.

Luke The Evangelist: The feast day of the companion of St. Paul and his biographer is celebrated on October 18th throughout the Catholic Church. Luke, who is presumed to have come from Antioch or Philippi, composed the third Gospel and the Acts of the Apostles. He is the patron saint of painters.

Luther: In Germany many Protestant Christian groups observe *Martinsfest* as the festival of Martin Luther's birthday, November 10, 1483. See also *Reformation*.

Macabees: See *Hanukkah*.

Maceo: The anniversary of the death of General Maceo, a national holiday in Cuba, celebrated the 7th of December. General Antonio Maceo, Calixto García and José Marti were the three great national heroes who, renewing Cuba's struggle against Spain, finally broke Spanish oppression in 1898, the year in which the United States officially allied herself with the Cuban struggle.

Magha Puja: February 28th. Festival of All Saints in Buddhism.

Magi: See *Epiphany*.

Makara Sankranti: The holiday celebrating the Hindu New Year of the winter season. The four New Year celebrations are observed at the beginning of each of the four seasons; *Makara Sankranti*, at the winter solstice, is especially important. It is a time of the great bathing festival at the River Ganges, celebrated when the sun enters the constellation of the House of Capricorn. Hindu astronomers refer to this sign of the zodiac as the Alligator; thence the name "Makara," which means "Alligator." See *Hindu Holidays*.

Makha Buja: The festival and season observed in Thailand, in our month of February, by pilgrimages to Phra Buddha Bath and other holy Buddhist shrines.

Mar Girgis: Celebration of the festival of St. George in the Coptic Church during Aarmuda (April).

Mardi Gras: Mardi Gras, on Shrove Tuesday, refers, by

association, to the carnival festival preceding Lent. Among Shrove Tuesday customs in France was the practice of leading a fatted ox through the streets; the name "Mardi Gras" is presumably derived from this source. It has, however, become associated almost entirely with the New Orleans festival instituted in 1857.

Marine Corps: November 10th is the anniversary of the organization of the United States Marine Corps when, in 1775, the Continental Congress authorized the formation of "two battalions of marines . . . consisting of one colonel, two lieutenant colonels, two majors, and other officers as usual in other regiments." On November 28th John Hancock appointed Samuel Nicholas of Philadelphia the Corps's first captain and charged him with the duty of recruiting.

Maritime: National Maritime Day was established in 1923. May 22nd was chosen in commemoration of the sailing of the *Savannah* in 1819, the first steamship successfully to cross the ocean.

St. Mark The Evangelist: April 25th marks the anniversary of the death of St. Mark in 75 A.D. The occasion is celebrated with particular significance in Venice, the city of which Mark is the patron saint. The companion of Paul and author of the second Gospel, St. Mark is believed to have founded the church at Alexandria. During the Middle Ages his feast day, then known as Litania Major was the occasion for the singing of four great litanies.

St. Mark's Eve was popular in England, especially among the common folk, for many customs and superstitions surrounded it.

Marlborough: The province of Marlborough, New Zealand, celebrates its territorial anniversary in public celebrations on November 1st, or the Monday nearest that date.

St. Martin: Born in 316, by profession a soldier, remarkably successful as an "Apostle to the Gauls," and gentle in all things, St. Martin was a popular Christian Father of the Church, both in his own time and in tradition. Martinmas, or the Feast of St. Martin, came, during the Middle Ages, to be a festive day throughout most of central and eastern Europe and England. It is celebrated November 11th.

Martyrdom of Hazrat Imam Husain: See *Muharram.*

Maryland: The 25th of March is observed as a state holiday in Maryland in memory of the safe arrival of Lord Baltimore's colonists in 1634 and the first Catholic Mass which they celebrated on that date.

Maryland Defenders: The anniversary of the bombardment of Fort McHenry in the War of 1812, which inspired Francis Scott Key to write "The Star Spangled Banner," is a bank holiday in Baltimore. The successful defense of Fort McHenry kept the British from capturing Baltimore on September 12th, 1814.

Maslyanitza: See *Butter Week.*

Mass: Since the Reformation the term has come to apply almost exclusively to the eucharistic service of thanksgiving and sacrifice performed in the Catholic service. The term is derived from the dismissal of the morning service performed in the Roman Catholic Church—specifically from the pronouncement *"Ite, missa est."* The use of the term, especially during the late Middle Ages, implied also the special festival or service being celebrated.

St. Matthew: September 21st, the feast day of Matthew, who wrote the first book of the New Testament, has been celebrated since the first days of the Christian Church. The Greek Orthodox Church celebrates his feast day on November 16th.

St. Matthias: One of the followers of Christ who had witnessed his baptism and the resurrection. Matthias was later chosen to take the place of the traitor Judas. His feast day is celebrated especially by the Eastern Church, on August 9th, in the Western on the last day of February.

Maulid: An Egyptian term corresponding roughly to celebration or, in practice, corresponding to a Christian saint day as observed in Europe. Essentially religious in nature, the festivities of the Moulid have, like those of the saint days, become associated with secular forms. Somewhere between the

13th and 15th centuries Moulids became a national institution in Egypt, though actually, as with some Christian holidays, they may themselves be the continuance of very ancient traditions. The date of the Moulid is, in most cases, determined by the Moslem lunar calendar. The festival has always been related to particular events or places and so is seldom celebrated with any degree of uniformity in Islam. See *Moslem Holidays*.

Maulid An-Nabi: The Birthday of the True Prophet is celebrated by all faithful of Islam about the eleventh day of the third Moslem month, Rabi *'ul-aw'wal*. Celebrations continue for nine days and fall on the anniversary of Mohammed's death rather than his birth, since the latter date is unknown.

Maundy Thursday: The Thursday before Easter and, therefore, a day of preparation for Easter. The word *Maundy* is presumably derived from *mandatum*. From medieval times the ceremony of the washing of the feet has been performed in commemoration of Jesus's having washed the feet of his disciples shortly before his crucifixion. Maundy is derived from *"dies mandati"* or *"*Mandate." In England once called Sheer Thursday, in the Greek faith Great Thursday.

May: Derived from the name of the goddess Maia and related to ancient Roman customs, our May Day takes its traditions from medieval England where, on May Day, the people returned from gathering may to dance about the maypole.

May Day Eve, April 30th, has been a popular holiday for folk traditions, which vary according to local customs and early history. In Czechoslovakia fires were lit on the hillsides to burn out the witches; in Finland it is a popular holiday celebrating the return of light.

McHenry: See *Maryland Defenders*.

McKinley: McKinley's birthday, January 29th, is an anniversary of local observance previously known as Carnation Day, still celebrated by certain Masonic lodges.

Meat Fare Sunday: See *Carnival*.

Mecklenburg: Mecklenburg Day has, since 1831, been a state holiday in North Carolina. The occasion marks the resolutions adopted May 20, 1775, which declared residents of Mecklenburg County, North Carolina, to be free of British rule. The wording of these resolutions, though subsequently lost, is said to be similar to that of the Declaration of Independence.

Meiji Setsu: Meiji Setsu celebrates, on the 3rd of November, the birthday of the Emperor Meiji Tenno who made his country a modern nation, who abolished feudalism and introduced modern industrial methods of work.

Memorial: See *Decoration Day*.

Memphis Cotton Carnival: First held in 1931 at Memphis, Tennessee, the Cotton Carnival has become a major fiesta in the South.

Merdeka: On August 31st Malay became an independent member of the British Commonwealth. Merdeka is Malayan Independence Day.

Mexico: The anniversary of the promulgation of both the Constitution of 1857 and that of 1917 is celebrated in Mexico on February 5th. The latter Constitution grew out of the 1910 Revolution, the former embodied liberal reforms carried to victory through the efforts of Benito Juárez. The anniversary of the Revolution is celebrated as a separate holiday on November 20th. See *Revolution of 1910* and *Juárez*.

Fiestas Patrias, or anniversary of Mexico's independence from Spain, is a great celebration lasting from two days to a week. It usually is climaxed on the 15th and 16th of September. On September 15, 1810 Father Miguel Hidalgo y Costilla gave the great freedom cry, the *"grito,"* which began the revolt in the town of Dolores.

Michaelmas: The feast day of St. Michael, September 29th, is celebrated by the English and Western Catholic Churches. Michael is mentioned five times in the Bible and each time as fighting heavenly battles. Michael, the Archangel, is patron of the Basque people and of many towns and cities, but his special province is the souls of all who are in Purgatory or on earth. In England, Michaelmas marks the beginning of one of the quarters of the fiscal year.

Mid-Lent: See *Laundresses*. It was formerly the custom in

central Europe to break the Lenten fast with a mid-Lent celebration, especially in Belgium and parts of France, called
Mothering Sunday in England.

Midsummer: The day of the summer solstice, as of the
winter solstice, has been observed since prehistoric times. Part
of the traditional rites performed in pre-Christian Europe,
notably among Teutonic and Scandinavian people, came down
to us in the custom of lighting St. John's fires on this day and
burning a Yule log at Christmas. See *St. John the Baptist* and
St. John's Eve.

Milky Way: See *Chi Hsi,* Chinese Festival of the Milky
Way.

Missouri: The first Monday in October, approved by the
state legislature in 1915 as the time for taking special note
of the state history. Observed locally in Missouri, as a holiday
in some parts of the state, the day has not been legally
adopted.

Mohammed: See *Maulid en-Nabi.*

Moon's Birthday: See *T'ai Yin.*

Mormon: See Pioneer Day.

Moses: Followers of Mohammed, especially in Palestine,
celebrate *'Id Nebi Mussa,* the Feast of the Prophet Moses,
usually with a procession leading from the shrine of Moses
near Jericho into Jerusalem.

Moslem Holidays: The variety of holidays celebrated by
followers of Mohammed cannot be too much stressed. Of
these perhaps the New Year (Muharram) is celebrated with
the greatest consistency throughout Islam, and certain other
holidays are universally observed. Maulid an-Nabi is one of
these, for it is the Prophet's birthday and *the* outstanding festival or Maulid of the year (see *Maulid*). Observance of Ramadan, with its attendant special functions and feast days, is a
basic pillar of the Faith. (See *Ramadan.*) In addition, a great
number of festivals such as 'Id al-Adha or 'Id al-Fitr celebrate traditional and religious stories about a great variety
of people, some of whom are the Prophet's spiritual successors,
many of whom are stellar figures in other religions. The latter
include nearly all the principals in the Old Testament, the

New Testament, the Jatakas and other religious works, including, of course, the Koran. All Moslem holidays are determined according to the lunar calendar, each year having 354 days. Islam, like most religions, is supranational. The progression of holidays is not, however, coordinated by a central controlling agency like the Roman Catholic Church during the Middle Ages. The majority of Maulids, or festivals, are, therefore, subject to complex factors which make it difficult to isolate representative holidays or to present an exact picture of such a variety of festivals.

Mother: The second Sunday in May is accepted throughout the country as Mother's Day. The date was originated by Miss Anna Jarvis who, through her perseverance, organized national and international interest in establishing this date. In many places in Europe St. Anne's Day provided occasion for honoring mothers.

Mother Cabrini: Mother Cabrini is the popular title for St. Frances Xavier Cabrini, virgin and foundress, and the first American citizen to be canonized as a saint. Her feast day is celebrated December 22nd.

Mothering Sunday: The mid-Sunday of Lent, the fourth Sunday of the Lenten period, was, in England, known as Mothering Sunday. At this time special cakes and presents were given mothers, as on our Mother's Day. Despite its position on the Christian calendar there is some reason to believe that Mothering Sunday had its origins in pre-Christian British traditions.

Muharram: The first ten days of the Muharram, the first month of the Moslem year, are dedicated to the mourning and remembrance of the martyrdom of Hezret Imam Husain, maternal grandson of the Prophet and son of Hazrat Ali and Fatima. Muharram is both the name of this first lunar month and of the ten-day celebration which also marks the beginning of the Moslem New Year.

Mumping: See *St. Thomas.*

Nanak: See *Guru Nanak* and *Sikh Holidays.*

Narali Purnima: The Hindu holiday of the full-moon day of Sravan in July or August. In the Bombay Presidency of

India the festival and fairs celebrating this occasion are held along the seashore, and offerings of coconuts are thrown into the ocean. Therefore the day is sometimes called Narali Purnima ("Coconut Full-Moon Day") but otherwise known as Raksha-Bandhan.

Narcissus: Chinese New Year's celebrations are popularly known in the Territory of Hawaii as Narcissus Festival. See *Ch'u Hsi.*

Nathan B. Forrest: The birthday of Nathan B. Forrest, soldier and great Confederate leader, is observed each year by Tennessee on July 13th. Forrest's heroism and military brilliance earned him a place of honor among Confederate statesmen and military leaders.

Nationale: See *Fête Nationale* or *Bastille Day.*

Nativity of the Virgin Mary: The feast day honoring the nativity of the mother of Jesus has been celebrated since the seventh century, if not earlier, and, to this day, by Roman and Eastern Catholic Churches and the Church of England. Parents of the Virgin Mary were Sts. Joachim and Anne.

Nauruz: Also called Navruz, the Parsi New Year, at which time, late in March, the followers of Zarathustra reaffirm the doctrine of Asha or piety, by which man fights against the force of evil (Angra Manyu) to attain the blessed state of Ahura Mazda (good). See *Zarathustra.*

Navy: A report by a special committee of the Continental Congress on October 27, 1775, marks the first official action taken in the establishment of the United States Navy. This date coincided with the birthday of Theodore Roosevelt who, as Assistant Secretary of the Navy and later as President, played an active role in Navy history. This date was chosen as the occasion of paying tribute to the exploits of the Navy. President Harding, in 1922, made the first formal motion to this effect.

Nelson: The province of Nelson, New Zealand, celebrates its territorial anniversary in public festivities each February 1st, or Monday nearest that date.

New Hampshire Fast: New Hampshire is the only state still to observe a fast as a legal holiday. This day of prayer for good harvests has been set aside for many years as an occasion complementary to the autumnal Thanksgiving Day. It is customarily called, by order of the governor, to fall on the fourth Thursday in April, though the state legislature abolished obligatory observance of the day in 1895.

New Orleans, Anniversary of the Battle of: General Andrew Jackson's victory at New Orleans on January 8, 1815, closed the gateway to the Mississippi Valley and effectively repulsed the British invasion of West Florida and Louisiana. The date is more generally remembered than celebrated, but has, throughout the South, been the occasion for festivals and holidays. It is a legal holiday in Louisiana.

New Year: Every calendar has its own New Year. Older traditions suggest the practice, still found among the Hindus, of observing seasonal New Year celebrations. Traces of four "natural New Years" appear in the Jewish lunar calendar and in Chinese morphology. The Greeks once began their New Year with the first new moon after June 21st, and the Romans before Julius Caesar on March 1st.

About 45 B.C. Julius Caesar adopted a plan whereby alternate months should have thirty-one days, beginning in Januarius, and all others thirty, thereby making a total of 366 days every four years. The extra day, which in leap year was nicely accommodated in February, was otherwise left out, giving February twenty-nine days, except on leap year. Later Augustus Caesar had the eighth month, Sextilis, named after himself. Not wishing his month to suffer by comparison with his predecessor's, he robbed another day from February so that August too would be equal to July.

Eventually, however, an error appeared in Caesar's calendar: natural time dropped behind the Julian calculation. In 1582, Pope Gregory found that the vernal equinox, instead of falling correctly on the 21st of March (as it had at the Council of Nicaea in 325) had rushed ahead to the 11th of that month. Gregory therefore decreed that October 5th of that year should be reckoned the 15th and that the first year of each century that could be divided by four should not be counted a leap year.

The Gregorian calendar was immediately adopted by all Catholic countries, with the sole exception of Russia, which was under the sway of the Eastern Church. Henry VIII having removed his state from papal jurisdiction, England persisted in the Julian style until 1752, when, by act of Parliament, the discrepancy, which then amounted to eleven days, was overtaken. The 3rd of September, that year, was reckoned the 14th; it was also agreed that three of every four centurial years should not be accounted a leap year. Because 1800 was not a leap year, the discrepancy between the new and old style calendars is now equivalent to twelve days. Thus in Russia, where the old style still obtains, principal holidays such as New Year's, Christmas or Easter, fall on the thirteenth day after the event is celebrated in other Christian countries.

January 1st is a legal holiday in all states and territories of the United States.

New Years for Trees: One of the four "natural New Years" of the Jewish lunar calendar, and not a religious celebration, the New Year for Trees was shifted to the fifteenth of the month of Shebat. On this day the sap is said to rise in the trees in the Holy Land in proof of the divine promise of abundance as long as the people of Israel kept His commandments. In modern Zionist Israel the 15th of Shebat is occasion for tree-planting (Arbor Day).

St. Nicholas: One of the most popular of all Christian saints, St. Nicholas is regarded as the patron of Russia, virgins, children and sailors; at other times, of clerks and scholars. Made Bishop of Myra in Lycia in the fourth century, St. Nicholas was, during his lifetime, noted for his benevolent acts and munificence. His feast day has, ever since, been associated with the giving of presents in some form. In Western Europe it is celebrated December 6th. Christmas festivities traditionally, throughout central and northern Europe, begin on St. Nicholas' Eve. Anniversary of the founding of the St. Nicholas Society by Washington Irving is annually celebrated on St. Nicholas Day in New York.

Night Watch: *La Retraite aux Flambeaux*, the eve of the anniversary of the Fall of the Bastille, July 13th, used to be celebrated in Paris with a procession of torchbearers, bands and lanterns.

Niiname-Sai: The second Japanese harvest festival, held November 23rd, at which the Emperor partakes of the new grain, together with his ancestors, and the people rejoice in the harvest. See *Kanname-Sai*, the first festival.

Ninth of Ab: See *Ab*.

Nisan: The first day of Nisan, the first sacred and seventh civil month of the Jewish calendar, is now considered the Jewish New Year. Originally it was one of four seasonal New Year feasts. See also *Tishri*, *Ab*, and *New Year for Trees*.

No: The anniversary of Greek rejection of the Fascist Italian ultimatum of 1940 was, for a number of years after the last war, celebrated as a major national holiday in modern Greece. It was called "No Day."

Noah's Sailing: See *Ashura*.

Norway: Norwegian independence is celebrated on May 17th (*Syttende Mai*) in commemoration of the adoption of the Norwegian constitution in 1814, formulated at Eidsvold in 1814.

Nutcracker Night: North of England term for Halloween.

Oberndorf: Each year the carol "Silent Night, Holy Night" is sung, in many languages, at Oberndorf, for it was here, in 1818, that the custodian of St. Nicola gave to the organist Joseph Mohr the poem which the latter set to music. Singing of this carol, which is known in so many tongues, has attracted international attention.

O-Bon: The Japanese Feast of Lanterns, comparable to the Chinese Festival of Lanterns, or Teng Chieh. The lanterns used in traditional ceremonies on this occasion symbolically light the path so that the spirits of the dead may return again to earth for the celebration. Graves of the dead are tended with special care on O-Bon.

Oklahoma: April 22nd in Oklahoma commemorates the date on which in 1889 the new land was opened for white settlement. The day is an optional holiday, at the governor's discretion, known as Oklahoma Historical Day.

St. Olaf: Olsok, the anniversary of St. Olaf's Day, cele-

brated July 29th. As a king, Olaf made many expeditions to
England, fought against the Danes there and, later, fought
with Cnute the Great. St. Olaf ruled betwen 1015 and 1028;
he introduced Christianity into his country and united the
kingdom; he is the patron saint of Norway.

Old Candlemas: See *Valentine's Day*, which falls on the
day which, before the change of style, was Candlemas Day,
and so derives this alternate name in some parts of England.

Old Christmas: January 6th, before change of style, was
reckoned Christmas; hence this date, now Epiphany (or
Twelfth Day) is still known as Old Christmas Day. In Russia
and wherever else the Julian calendar still obtains, Christmas
is celebrated on January 6th.

Old Hickory: See *Jackson's Day*.

Old Year's: Variant of New Year's Eve.

Olsok: See *St. Olaf*.

Omer: Omer, meaning "sheaf," refers to the seven weeks
of the Jewish religious calendar between Passover and Pentecost. The seven full weeks (Lev. 23:15) of the harvest period
are observed, like the Christian Lent, as a period during which
normal social activities are suspended or curtailed. Restrictions are, however, relaxed for Lag b'Omer, a traditional folk
holiday (which see).

Omisoka: Japanese Old Year's Day is, like the comparable
Chinese holiday, Ch'u Hsi, a time for settling accounts as well
as celebrating the old year out.

Orange: Irish Protestants still locally celebrate the triumph
of Protestant forces in Ireland at the Battle of Boyne, July 12,
1690. After William of Orange had been made king of England in 1689, Irish Catholics joined forces against his sup-
porters in Ireland and were defeated in this encounter.

Orange Bowl Week: December 25th through January 3rd
has for some years been a successful state- and civic-sponsored
fiesta week in Miami, Florida, culminating in the annual
Orange Bowl Parade.

Oshogatsu: Japanese New Year's Day, a national and religious holiday; the spirits of the dead are said to be present
on this day, and Japanese history and tradition of the past

are especially meaningful. The imperial household observes the rites of Shihohai.

St. Oswald: A minor feast day (August 5th) especially of the Anglican Church originating in Anglo-Saxon times. St. Oswald, King of the Northumbrians, succeeded to the throne in 634; his great charity and heroism are described by the Venerable Bede.

Otago: The provinces of Otago and Southland, New Zealand, celebrate their territorial anniversaries in public celebrations on March 23rd, or the Monday nearest that date.

Our Lady of Lourdes: February 11th, the feast of Our Lady of Lourdes, commemorates the first of the many apparitions of the Virgin Mary to St. Bernadette in the year 1858.

Our Lady of St. Carmel: July 16th is the principal feast day of what is probably the oldest mendicant order of the Roman Church; the fiesta may last several days. While the feast itself was instituted about 1380, the order traces its origin to the time of the prophet Elias, who built an altar on Mount Carmel.

Pajjusana: The Great Fast of *Pajjusana* is observed by Jains in India one month and twenty nights after the end of the rainy season. This is a time of purification and special prayers among a people which live so as never to hurt any living thing.

Pakistan: Commemorating the inception of Pakistan as an independent nation in 1947, August 14th is the great national patriotic holiday of Pakistan.

Pakistan's Republic Day, March 23rd, celebrating the declaration of Pakistan as an independent republic in 1956, is also an important national holiday.

Palio: The *Festa del Palio* or horse race, held twice each year at Siena, is one of the great traditional fetes of Italy. This great race has been run approximately on the 2nd of July and the 16th of August since the fourteenth century.

Palm Sunday: Properly known as the Second Sunday of the Passion, this is the first Sunday in Lent and the first day in the Holy Week which immediately precedes Easter. Palm Sunday celebrates Christ's triumphal entry into Jerusalem. It derives its name from the palm branches, symbolic of peace, which were waved on that occasion. Representation of the scene was very popular during the Middle Ages. The date when it was first celebrated is not known.

Pan-American: April 14th is observed by twenty-one American republics in honor of the creation of the Pan-American Union in 1890. President Hoover, in 1931, made the first request for official observance by the United States.

Pancake Tuesday: See *Shrove Tuesday*. Of the various national festivities associated with this day, the English custom of eating pancakes prevails to the modern day.

Paraguay: Paraguay declared herself independent from Spain on August 14, 1811, and this date is celebrated as the anniversary of her independence.

Paraskeve: The Day of Preparation, or Friday, in the Mosaic tradition of strict observance of the Sabbath as prescribed for early Christians and, to this day, for Orthodox Jews.

Parsee: See *Zarathustra*.

Pasch: The ceremony of sprinkling the blood of the sacrificial lamb upon the lintels and doorposts of the house observed in the Jewish Passover. In Christian theology the significance of the ceremony is associated with the celebration of Holy Communion. See *Passover*.

Passion: The Passion is generally used to signify the suffering of Christ and the crucifixion or, in a more explicit sense, the ecumenical re-enactment which is performed on Good Friday. (See *Good Friday*.) Passion Week is the full week before Holy Week, the last week of Lent in the Catholic calendar. Passion Sunday is the Sunday immediately preceding Easter and, by count, the sixth Sunday of Lent, or the sixth Quadragesima Sunday.

Passover: The Jewish Feast of the Unleavened Bread, originally instituted in Egypt in commemoration of the redemption of Israel (Exodus 23:15, Deut. 16:16). On this night the Lord smote the first-born of all of the land of Egypt except of the houses of the Israelites, who had sprinkled the blood of the sacrificial lamb upon their doorposts. This ceremony, the *pesah,* was actually of earlier origin (Ex. 12:43), initiating a six-day seasonal festival called the Feast of the Unleavened Bread, but it coincided with Jehovah's smiting the first-born of Egypt. The word *"pesah"* or *"skip"* was connected with the original significance of the observance, and the significance of the Passover therefore partakes of the theme of redemption or release from spiritual bondage, release from physical bondage (in Egypt), and of the seasonal release from winter's toils. The Passover is begun on the evening of the 14th of Nisan, the first sacred month of the Jewish calendar, with a sacrificial meal, and is celebrated as a major feast on the 15th of Nisan, between April 4th and 14th.

In Christian theology, Christ is the Paschel Lamb of the New Testament. His appearance on earth and sacrifice were pre-figured by the paschal lamb—and Passover—of the Old Testament. The Eucharist (Mass) is intimately related, in Roman Catholic circles, to this sacrifice.

St. Patrick: The festival on March 17th (also called Shamrock Day) honoring the patron saint of Ireland is especially dear to the hearts of the Irish. Born in the fifth century in Ireland, Patrick spent a number of years preparing himself for missionary work among his own people and, after training on the Continent, returned to Ireland to commence his most successful endeavors. He opposed Druidical worship and succeeded in converting some twelve thousand persons to Christianity.

Patriots: A state holiday in Maine and Massachusetts to commemorate the Battle of Lexington and Concord, April 19, 1775.

St. Paul: See *Conversion of St. Paul* and *Peter and Paul.*

Pearl Harbor: Upon the Japanese attack on Pearl Harbor in the city of Honolulu, December 7, 1941, the United States declared war on Japan and her allies. The anniversary of this day is variously observed by patriotic and military groups in the U.S.

Peggy Stewart: A local and not a legal anniversary in Maryland, observed on October 19th, especially at Annapolis, to celebrate the burning of the ship *Peggy Stewart* and its cargo of tea. A public meeting ordered the owners to sign a confession of guilt for having brought the tea into the harbor. To expiate the sentiment aroused, Anthony Stewart, the owner, himself set fire to the *Peggy Stewart*.

Pennsylvania: On the anniversary of the birthday of William Penn, October 24, 1644 (adjusted to the new calendar), the state of Pennsylvania celebrates the founding of the state, its history and the memory of its founder. The day was set aside by legislative action on June 22, 1931.

Pentecost: For the Christian celebration of the feast of Pentecost, see *Whitsunday;* for the Jewish tradition, see *Weeks*.

Perchtenlauf: In Austria, especially in the Tyrol, the tradition of Perchten masks and dances to scare winter away predates Christian times, but it has become associated with folk festivals observed on or just after Epiphany.

Peru: Peru declared her independence from Spain on July 28, 1821.

Pesah: See *Passover*.

Peter and Paul: The Feast of St. Peter and St. Paul, "Princes of the Apostles," was from the fifth century, celebrated as a holy day of obligation on June 29th. It is so observed today in the Greek Orthodox Church. The ceremony, however, was divided in the sixth century, to facilitate the performance of the service at St. Peter's in Rome. St. Paul's Mass is now celebrated on June 30th in the Western Church. St. Peter, who carries the Keys of the Kingdom, and St. Paul, especially venerated by theologians, were both put to death about the year 64 in the reign of Nero. St. Peter is acknowledged the chief of the apostles and is, by the Catholic Church, considered the vicar of Christ on earth, for he was the apostle to whom Christ gave the primacy.

Petofi: March 15th is the birthdate of Sándor Petöfi, Hungarian national poet and patriot. The national holiday on this occasion is of great importance in Hungary. Petöfi led students in the 1848 rebellion against the Hapsburg Empire.

Philip: One of the twelve apostles and, according to tradition, missionary to Phrygia, where he suffered martyrdom. His feast day is celebrated by the Byzantine Church on November 14, by the Roman Catholic Church on May 11th.

Pig: See *Killing the Pigs*.

Pilgrimage: In the best sense, the Pilgrimage to Mecca is a true holiday of Islam, which comes to fortunate believers only once during their lifetime. The ritual of the Pilgrimage is described in the Koran. It is the fifth Pillar of the Faith. See *Moslem Holidays*.

Pilgrimage to Puri: See *Procession of the Chariots*.

Pilgrims: See *Forefathers*.

Pioneer: The anniversary of the founding of the first white settlement at Franklin, Idaho, on June 15, 1860, was made a legal holiday in Idaho in 1911; it is known as Pioneer Day. In quite a different sense Pioneer Day in Utah has religious as well as historical significance. Pioneer Day in Utah, July 24th, has been celebrated since 1849 and was made a legal holiday in 1882 in honor of the arrival of Brigham Young's party at the site of what is now Salt Lake City.

Plough Monday: The first Monday after the Twelfth Day of Christmas, at which time rural work was resumed after the Christmas holidays, an occasion marked, in medieval England, by jokes and festivities. Plough Monday dinner is traditionally celebrated by the Lord Mayor in London. See *St. Distaff's Day*, counterpart for women.

Poets: See *Collop Monday*.

St. Polycarp: Bishop of Smyrna, martyr and disciple of St. John the Evangelist. Feast day January 26th.

Ponce De Leon: Ponce de Leon's landing on Easter Sunday, 1513, at the site of present-day St. Augustine, Florida, is celebrated yearly in that city.

Poppy Week: During Poppy (or Buddy) Week, Veterans of Foreign Wars have annually sponsored the sale of poppies. The week ends the Saturday before Memorial Day.

Portugal: October 5th marks the establishment of the Portuguese Republic after the revolution of 1910; it is celebrated as a national holiday in Portugal. Restoration Day, December 1st, marks the end of the sixty years of captivity and crowning of John IV, Duke of Braganza on December 13, 1640, O.S. This too is a national holiday.

Posadas: *Las Posadas,* "the lodging," the name given in Mexico to the nine holy days of the Christmas season. The story of Mary and Joseph's night at the inn is retold in pageants and with little figures.

Posaha: Twice each month, on the new moon and the full moon, Jains observes the fast of Posaha, analogous to the Sabbath.

Poson: The full-moon fast and religious holiday among the Singhalese and Buddhists.

Presentation at the Temple: Candlemas, variously called "Purification," "The Coming of the Son of God into the Temple," "The Meeting of the Lord" (*Hypapante Kyriou*), and "The Feast of Simeon the Old Man" (*'Id Sham'oun al-Shaikh*). As prescribed by Mosaic law, Jesus was presented at the Temple forty days after Epiphany. (Luke 2:22 ff.) This service, conducted with candles and penitential prayers, was prescribed by Pope Sergius I in the eighth century. It is celebrated February 2nd. See *Candlemas* and *Purification.*

Pretorius: See *Covenant.*

Prima Sabbati: By Jewish reckoning Sunday was the first day after Sabbath and hence was called *prima Sabbati,* later adapted, in the Christian era, to the Day of the Lord and, still later, popularly known as Sun Day, or Sunday.

Procession of the Chariots: Each year devout Hindu pilgrims gather at Puri (also known as Jagannath or Juggernaut) on the Bay of Bengal to see the chariots of Krishna and his brother and sister carry the images of the gods from their winter to their summer home. The Procession of the Chariots is a ceremonious and holy Hindu occasion. See *Hindu Holidays.*

Prophet's Birthday: For the Prophet's Birthday, celebrated annually by the faithful of Islam, see *Maulid an-Nabi.*

Psychosabbaton: See *Saturday of the Souls.*

Puebla—Anniversary of the Battle of Puebla: May 5th marks one of the great Mexican national holidays celebrating the victory of Mexican forces over the French Army which sought to install Maximilian of Austria as Emperor. This battle was fought in 1862.

Pulaski: Certain states observe General Pulaski Memorial Day on October 11th. Pulaski joined Washington's Army in 1777. His greatest success was the defense of Charleston in May, 1779, with a corps known as the Pulaski Legion. He died in October of the same year.

Pure Brightness: See *Ch'ing Ming*, Chinese festival of the Pure and Bright.

Purification: Presentation of the Lord in the Temple is associated in Roman Catholic liturgy with the Purification of the Blessed Virgin Mary, also called Candlemas. This festival was established by Justinian and falls forty days after Epiphany. See *Candlemas*.

Purim: Festival of Purim, celebrated on the 14th day of Adar (March), the twelfth sacred month of the Jewish calendar, celebrates the deliverance of the Jews in Persia from a plot by the ruler Haman to destroy them (Esther 9:19-28). The name is derived from *"Pur,"* a lot cast to determine the day most propitious to Haman's scheme. The day is therefore known as the Feast of Lota. It roughly corresponds to the Christian Carnival season (Twelfth Night).

Quadrigesima: In the Catholic calendar, the beginning of the forty days' fast preceding Easter; hence this first Sunday is called Quadrigesima Sunday.

Quaid-I-Azam: Literally, "The Great Leader," Quaid-i-Azam was the title bestowed upon Mr. M. A. Jinnah, founder of Pakistan, whose death is memorialized on September 11th in Pakistan. His birthdate, December 25th, is also observed.

Queen's Birthday: Throughout Great Britain and in the dominions and territories of the British Empire the Queen's Birthday is celebrated as a national holiday.

Quinquagesima Sunday: The fiftieth day before (and including) Easter; therefore, the first Sunday before Ash Wednesday, the Sunday before Lent.

Quinto-Feira Da Espiga: Among the Portuguese the fortieth day after Easter celebrates the harvest of olives, wheat, flowers and herbs. It is, especially, a folk holiday, though national in character.

Rage: The anniversary of Columbus' discovery of the New World, October 12th, Columbus Day in the United States, is called *Dia de la Raza,* or the Day of the Race, in Spanish America. It was Columbus' discovery which made possible a new race, a fusion of Spanish and Indian blood.

Raksha-Bandhan: A Hindu holiday celebrating the full-moon day of Sravan in July or August. Also called Narali Purnima. The name "Raksha-Bandhan" is derived from the *"rakhi"* or amulet worn by brothers and sisters as a charm to protect them from evil during the ensuing year. See *Narali Purnima.*

Ram Lila: Each day during the Hindu festival of the Divine Goddess Durga is presented a pageant called the Ram Lila. Based on the epic *Ramayana,* this story tells of the victory of Rama (seventh incarnation of the Lord Vishnu) over the demon Ravana, who treatened to enslave both mankind and the gods above.

Rama: Anniversary of the birth of Rama, incarnation of Vishnu, is celebrated by Hindus on the first day of Chaitra in March or April. The celebration lasts nine days; it is called Ramnavani.

Ramadan: During the thirty days of Ramadan, the ninth month of the Mohammedan calendar, the faithful of Islam observe a strict fast, from sunrise to sundown. This was the month during which Mohammed received divine revelations. Ramadan corresponds to the Christian Lent. Observance of Ramadan is one of the five great tenets of Islam. At its end is celebrated *'Id al-Fitr,* which see.

Ramavani: See *Rama.*

Ratha Yathra: The holiday celebrating the Hindu New Year which begins the summer season. At this time the Lord Vishnu changes from his winter to his summer home. See *Hindu Holidays.*

Raza: See *Race.*

Redemption: The feast of the Precious Blood (or Most Precious Blood of our Lord Jesus Christ) is celebrated in the

Roman Catholic Church as a feast of redemption commemorating the crucifixion with a special feast day on July 1st.

Reformation: In the Lutheran Church October 31st, or the Sunday nearest, is celebrated as the beginning of the Protestant Reformation, for it was on All Saints' Eve, 1517, that Martin Luther posted his 95 theses on the door of the Schlosskirche at Wittenberg,

Rejoicing-in-the-Law: The second day of the Festival of Azereth is known as the festival of Rejoicing-in-the-Law, celebrating the mystical marriage of Israel to the Law. See *Azereth* and *Tabernacles*.

Remembrance: Canadian Armistice Day, November 11th.

Remedios: The Fiesta of the Virgin of los Remedios is held the first week of September in the city of Los Remedios, Mexico. There the image of the Virgin, reputed to have been brought to Mexico by Cortes, is the center of the festival. During the War for Independence the Virgin de Los Remedios was patron saint of the Spanish armies.

Republic: The Day of the Republic is a principal national holiday in Italy commemorating the Referendum of June 2, 1946, which abolished the monarchy.

Repudiation of the Stamp Act: An occasion celebrated on November 23rd in Frederick, Maryland, in honor of the order of court of Frederick County denying the legality of the stamped paper which British occupation required.

Retraite aux Flambeaux: See *Night Watch*.

Revolution of 1910: The anniversary of the Mexican Revolution of 1910 is celebrated, in conjunction with the Revolution of 1810, on Mexican Constitution Day. But on the 20th of November it is especially remembered. The Revolution, led by Porfirio Diaz, overthrew the feudalistic structure of Mexican society and gave the land to the Mexican people.

Rhododendron: Since 1928 the blossoming of the rhododendron has been occasion for a festival held the middle of June at Asheville, North Carolina.

Riley: The birthday of James Whitcomb Riley, "the Hoosier Poet," was the occasion of public observances as early as 1912. Riley died in 1916, but the pleasantry of his verse won him many friends, and his birthday, October 7th, is frequently marked by local tributes in Indiana public schools and civic organizations.

Rivera: The birthday of Luis Muñoz Rivera, popularly styled "Puerto Rico's own George Washington," is celebrated on July 17th. Rivera, the first Resident Commissioner in Washington, D.C., was born in Barranquitas and is the father of Governor Rivera.

St. Roche: The feast day of Saint Roche, patroness of the sick, is celebrated throughout Italy but especially in Florence, where a flower festival is held in her honor on August 16th.

Rock Day: "Rock" being another term for "distaff," St. Distaff's Day was sometimes called Rock Day.

Rogation: Public feast days of the Latin Church on the Monday, Tuesday and Wednesday before Ascension Day (Holy Thursday). Special litanies or rogations for these days presumably originated in Vienna in the fifth century, at a time of peril to the city from earthquake and fire. They invoke God's blessing on man's temporal projects and nature's benevolence. The Sunday preceding is called Rogation Sunday, ushering in Rogation Week. The feast of St. Mark, April 25th, is the Greater Rogation Day.

Rogers: Will Rogers, "Oklahoma's best-known son," is honored with an optional holiday on November 4th, the anniversary of his birth in 1879.

Roosevelt: The birthday of Franklin Delano Roosevelt, born January 30, 1882, is observed in Kentucky as a state holiday.

St. Rosalia: The Feast of St. Rosalia, whose relics in 1625 were reputed to have stopped the ravages of the Black Death in Palermo, is a great festival each year (5th through 15th of July). St. Rosalia is the patroness of Palermo.

Rose: Rose festivals are held locally in many villages of France. In the United States the most widely known is the Rose Festival in Portland, Oregon, which has been celebrated annually since 1907.

St. Rose of Lima: The 30th of August was appointed by Pope Clement X as a special festival for Rose of Lima, whom he canonized for her especially devout and pious life. Rose of Lima was born in Peru in 1586. Her feast day is observed throughout Peru.

Rosh Ha-Shanah: One of the four seasonal New Years of the Jewish calendar, being celebrated the first of the month of Tishri. Rosh Ha-shanah has become the religious New Year; it is also called the Blowing of the Trumpet, or the Day of Memorial, or the Day of Judgment. On this day all creatures pass before the eyes of God to be judged.

Rosh Ha-shanah falls on the first day of the interlunar month of Tishri, the first civil and seventh sacred month of the Jewish calendar. It falls, by Gregorian count, in September or October. The Day of Blowing of the Trumpet marks the first day of a period of fast which lasts until the Day of Atonement, Yom Kippur, the second great solemn day of the Jewish faith. Biblical reference (Num. 29:1) would suggest that the 1st of Tishri was perhaps a day of memorial in commemoration of the dead. But additive meanings stress the redemptive aspects of faith each year renewed.

Runeberg: The birthday of Finland's national poet, Johan Ludvig Runeberg, is celebrated as a national holiday, an occasion for patriotic sentiments as well as a festival of lighted torches placed around the poet's statue in Helsinki. Runeberg's poem *Vårt Land* was adopted for the national anthem.

Sabado de Gloria: See *Saturday of Glory*.

Sabbath: In the Judaeo-Christian tradition the divinely instituted day of rest, the seventh day, on which God rested after creating the world and all his work. Observance of the Sabbath dates far back into antiquity. Hebdomadal division of time was favored at least as early as the great flood, and it is possible that the name "Sabbath" was used in Assyria and Babylonia. Sabbath was not applied to the Christian Sunday (or *prima Sabbati*) until well after the Reformation when Puritans and Presbyterians adopted the custom.

Sacrifice: For the Festival of the Sacrifice, see *'Id al-Adha*.

Saints' Days: While there are innumerable Saints' Days, of both Western and Eastern Catholic churches, only a few are mentioned in this work. As patrons of a special parish, diocese or country, some saints' days may be observed with greater solemnity in one locality than elsewhere. Butler's *Lives of the Saints* contains over two thousand five hundred entries. The official book of Roman Martyrology lists a catalogue of saints and their feast days throughout the year. But in observance, religious and secular elements are frequently intermingled in the feast days of canonized saints. Feasts are of several classifications, the major observances being universal throughout the Church. These include the feasts of the Blessed Trinity, of Our Lord, of the Blessed Virgin Mary, of St. Joseph, St. John the Baptist, the apostles, evangelists, and many confessors, martyrs and virgins.

Salvation Army: William Booth, founder and first General of the International Salvation Army, was born on August 10, 1829. His birthday is observed by Salvation Army groups in the United States and abroad.

San Jacinto: In Texas the anniversary of the Battle of San Jacinto is celebrated on April 12th, at the option of the governor of the state. On this day in 1836 General Sam Houston won a decisive victory over the Mexican Army, gaining independence for Texas.

Santa Fe: The first fiesta celebrating the reconquest of New Mexico was ordered by the Spanish governor Marquis de la Penuela in 1712. The custom fell into neglect and was not re-established until 1934. The governor's palace, built between 1610 and 1614 from material brought from Spain, provides the setting for historical features of the fiesta, held on September 1st.

Saturday: The day of the week sacred to Saturn, the Roman god of sowing and wheat. In many states of the U.S., Saturday is by statute a legal half-holiday.

Saturday of Glory: (*Sabado de Gloria.*) The Saturday before Easter is, in Mexico, observed as the anniversary of the hanging of Judas Iscariot. Horrible-looking effigies of the betrayor are hung amid general rejoicing.

Saturday of the Souls: In the Greek Orthodox Church prayers in memory of the spirits of departed saints and souls in Purgatory are reserved for the Saturday before Sexagesima

Sunday, called the Saturday of the Souls, or *Psychosabbaton.*
See *All Soul's Day.*

Saturnalia: This Roman celebration was extended, during
the time of the Empire, to a period of seven days, a festival
honoring Saturn, god of seed and sowing. Originally all military operations were stopped during this period, slaves were
temporarily freed, schools closed, presents were exchanged,
etc. The statue of Saturn—its feet were normally bound with
woolen bands to keep it from running away—was "set free" to
join in the festivities.

St. Sava: The feast day of Sveti Sava, national patron saint
of the Serbian peoples, falls on January 27th.

Schwenkfelder Thanksgiving: September 24th is a day of
thanksgiving for a small religious group in Pennsylvania who
found freedom in the New World. On this day, 1734, they first
gave thanks to God for it. Service is held in the Towamencin
Church for descendants or followers of Caspar von Schwenk-
feld, born in 1490, whose Protestant teachings and devout life
brought him a large following in his own lifetime.

Sechselauten: The "Six-O'clock-Ringing Feast" is an annual festival in Zurich to carry out winter and bring in summer, both in effigy and in a parade begun at six o'clock on an
appointed day in April.

Season of Freedom: Alternate and occasionally used term
for the Jewish Passover. See *Passover.*

Second Christmas: The day after Christmas. In the Netherlands and other Nordic countries many of the less religious
aspects of the Christmas celebration are reserved for Second
Christmas Day.

Second of May: *Dos de Mayo,* the Spanish observance of
the anniversary of the Citizens' Revolt in Madrid against
French rule in 1808. The ensuing battle began the War of
Mexican Independence.

Second Passover: On the 14th of Iyar (May), the second
lunar month of the Jewish sacred calendar, it was formerly
customary for persons who were unable to keep the first
Passover to observe a second.

Second Sunday After Epiphany: A day of obligation in

the Roman Catholic Church celebrating Christ's first recorded miracle, at the marriage feast at Cana. (John 2:1-11.)

Sempach: The anniversary of Austrian defeat at the Battle of Sempach, July 9, 1386, is a significant date in Swiss history. Many persons make a pilgrimage each year to the Battle Church at Sempach in honor of this occasion.

Senior Citizens: An optional holiday in Oklahoma, observed at the governor's proclamation on June 9th in honor of the elder citizens of this state. Known as Senior Citizens' Day.

Sepoy Mutiny: While the anniversary of the Sepoy Mutiny in India is not an official holiday, it is popularly celebrated in many parts of that country. The revolution, which began because Moslem and Hindu soldiers believed cartridges had been greased with animal fat, briefly restored Mogul rule and nearly ended British administration of the country in 1857.

Septuagesima Sunday: The third Sunday before Lent on the Roman Catholic calendar.

Settlers: Settlers' Day, a public holiday in the Union of South Africa commemorating the memory of early British pioneers who settled South Africa in September of 1820—and all other settlers who have arrived since that date.

Setsubun: The Japanese spring fete which takes place, by our calculations, in February. At this festival *mamemaki,* or bean-throwing, plays a prominent role. By this means evil spirits are driven away so that the crops will be good and the land prolific.

Seventeenth of Tammuz: See *Tammuz.*

Seward: In Alaska Seward (or Seward's) Day, March 30th, marks the occasion of the purchase of this Territory from Russia, negotiated by William Henry Seward in 1867. A territorial holiday.

Sexagesima: A "movable" holiday on the Roman Catholic calendar celebrated the second Sunday before Lent.

Shab-E-Barat: For Islam, a Day of Remembrance of the Dead analogous to the Christian All Souls' Day.

Shabuoth: The Jewish Feast of Weeks, originally an occasion for offering Jehovah an offering seven weeks after the beginning of the barley harvest (Deut. 16:9, 10). Gradually, however, the festival became associated with the children of Israel's arrival at Mount Sinai, as they fled Egypt, and Moses' receiving the Ten Commandments. Thus it gained the significance of "the season of the giving of our Law" and became, in a sense, the birthday of Israel. Spiritually, the Jewish Pentecost, it remains a major holiday of the Jewish faith. See *Weeks* and *Pentecost*.

Shamrock: See *St. Patrick*.

Sheelah: March 18th, the day after St. Patrick's Day, has traditionally been known as Sheelah's Day.

Sheer Thursday: See *Maundy Thursday*.

Sheker Bairam: In Turkey the three-day celebration which breaks the Fast of Ramadan, beginning therefore on the first day of the tenth lunar month of the Mohammedan calendar.

Shemini Azereth: The eighth day and the day of festival added to the seven-day Jewish festival of Succoth, or Rejoicing-in-the-Law. See Azereth and Succoth.

Shigoto Hajime: The second day of the year, celebrating the beginning the first work of the New Year, a popular Japanese festival. Observance varies with different parts of the country. This holiday is analogous to the English Plough Monday.

Shenandoah Valley Apple Blossom Festival: Begun in 1924 at the suggestion of a citizen of Winchester, Virginia, the festival has been held annually on May 3rd each year.

Shinnenenkai: The fifth day after the Japanese New Year's, at which time the first banquet is given at the Imperial Court.

Shivaratra: Hindu day of fasting in honor of the Lord Shiva, observed on the thirteenth day of each half of the month. The Shivaratri (Sivaratra) which falls within the dark period of Magh in January or February is especially sacred.

Shivaree: A U.S. colloquial custom of celebrating a marriage with general pandemonium, now fallen into disuse. The bridegroom was formerly required to appease the noisemakers by giving out cigars and other gifts.

Shri Panchami: See *Vasant Panchami*.

Shrove: Popular name for Quinquagesima Sunday is

Shrove Sunday, a term derived from the confession or "shrift" made in preparation for the beginning of Lent. In certain Nordic countries Shrove Monday is a popular holiday. Shrove Tuesday, the day before Ash Wednesday, was more generally a fete day in central Europe. In France Shrove Tuesday came to be called *mardi gras;* in England, Pancake Tuesday. See both.

Shuki-Korei-Sai: (Also Shumki-Korai-Sai.) The festival of the Vernal Equinox is observed in Japan as a national and religious holiday. See *Vernal Equinox.*

Sikh Holidays: The principal Sikh holiday is the birthday of the founder of the religion, Guru Nanak. But Guru Govind Singh's birthday, celebrated in December or January; Guru Arjun's Martyrdom Day, observed in May or June; and Guru Tegh Bahadur's Martyrdom Day in December are also noteworthy.

Silvester: In Austria New Year's Eve is popularly called "Silvester" or "Silvester's Eve."

Simeon: In the Orient the Christian Feast of Candlemas, celebrating the Presentation at the Temple, is known as the Feast of Simeon, who held Christ in his arms on this occasion.

Simhat Torah: The second day of the Jewish feast of Rejoicing-in-the-Law, known as Succoth, is called Simhat Torah. On this day special festivities and services celebrate joy in the Torah.

Simon: One of the twelve apostles, surnamed "the Cananean" and "the Zealous." Missionary, according to tradition, to Egypt and, later, to Persia, where he suffered martyrdom with St. Jude. His feast day is October 28th, or May 10th in the Eastern Church.

Six-Hour: Popular and semi-official term for Australia's Labor Day. Also called Eight-Hour Day. The first Monday in October was first called "Eight-Hour Day" before the forty-hour week was introduced in New South Wales.

Ski: For the international ski meet, see *Holmenkollen Day.*

Songkran: April 13th. Marks the beginning of the New Year in the Maha Sakaraj (solar) era. Libations of Water are poured to bathe the images of the Buddha, the Monks, the

parents and elders generally. This outpouring of water is one
of the oldest ceremonies of propitiation known. In village this
religious rite is apt to become a friendly combat of water
throwing.

Southland: See *Otago*.

Spring: Many cities, states and countries celebrate the first
day of spring in a manner determined by tradition and ancient
practice. In some areas Spring Day may correspond to a saint
day or other religious holiday. The Jewish Passover and
Christian Easter make significant the renaissance of life. St.
George's feast day (April 23rd) was associated with the
coming of spring, especially in countries which had contact
with early Christianity of the Eastern Catholic Church (Spain,
Poland, and even Austria). St. Anthony's Day, in Italy and
Portugal, had a similar association, but perhaps St. Vitus's
Day, June 15th, is the best known of the several saints' days
which mark the coming of spring. This was an especially
popular feast day in France, Germany, England, Scandinavia
and eastern Europe. See also *Yu Shui, Li Chum* and *Basanta*.

Statehood: Anniversary of the admission of Tennessee and
Kentucky into the Union is, in both states, known as Statehood Day and, in both states, is celebrated on June 1st. Kentucky became a state in 1792; Tennessee was admitted to the
Union in 1796.

St. Stephen: The feast day for Saint Stephen the "Pro-
Martyr" is established for December 26th. Stephen, the first
Christian martyr, was stoned to death a few years after the
death of Christ (in Acts 6, 7.). By some curious means St.
Stephen came at a very early date to be considered the patron
of horses. Throughout Europe and Scandinavia farm horses
were decorated and blessed on his feast day. In England this,
the first day after Christmas, is popularly called Boxing
Day.

The feast day of St. Stephen of Hungary, patron, King and
confessor, is celebrated on September 2nd throughout the
Western Church.

Stir-Up Sunday: The Sunday before Advent. U.S. slang.

Stonewall Jackson: The birthday of "Stonewall" Jackson

(January 21st) is celebrated in Virginia in connection with the anniversary of the birth of Robert E. Lee.

Store Bededag: The fourth Friday after Easter was established by Christian VII as a Danish holiday, a Great Day of Prayer.

Succoth: For the Jewish Feast of Booths, Succoth (or Succot), see *Tabernacles*.

Sun Dance: The ceremony known generally as the sun dance was performed by many American prairie Indian tribes at the budding of the wild sage. The dance itself, usually begun at sunrise, continued until the next daybreak.

Sun Festivals: In northern Norway especially, and in some southern parts of Scandinavia as well, public celebrations mark the first appearance of the summer sun after several months of winter darkness. For the Chinese celebration of the birthday of the Sun, the King of the Day, see *T'ai Yang*.

Sun Yat-Sen: Birthday of the famous leader of the Chinese Revolution in 1911 is celebrated March 12th. As first President of the Republic, Sun Yat-sen is also remembered on Chinese Independence Day, October 10th, observed in Republican China only.

Sunday: Sunday, the day following the Sabbath, was originally adopted by the apostles as an additional day of worship in memory of Christ's resurrection (Acts 20:7). According to St. Paul, observances of the Sabbath was not deemed obligatory for Gentiles, but for the early Christians, observance of the *prima Sabbati* had a function similar to the "Day of the Lord" or *kyriake*—the term still used by the Greek Church. Later the Roman name for the day, *Dies Solis*, was universally adopted.

Svetla Nedelya: The Week of Light the week following Easter, is, among the Bulgarians, an especially joyous season. It is the anniversary of the time when, according to tradition, the sun shone for eight days after Christ's resurrection.

Swallows: In central Europe the "Feast of the Swallows" (*Schwalbentag*) was a popular name for the Annunciation, for it was generally supposed that the swallows returned on this day, March 25th.

Swedenborg: On January 29th, members of the Church of New Jerusalem, or the New Church, which grew out of the teachings of Emanuel Swedenborg, celebrate the anniversary of the birth of their spritual leader, philosopher, writer and prophet.

Swedish Settlement: Anniversary of the arrival in America of the first Swedish colonists in 1638 is observed by many Swedish-American groups in the U.S. Early settlers landed on March 29th along the Delaware River.

St. Swithin: St. Swithin, Bishop of Winchester, was born about the year 800. He was never officially canonized by the Pope but earned the title "Saint" through the associations attached to his name. There is no record as to why St. Swithin's Day, July 15th, should have become such a popular occasion for weather predictions, except that this day, the anniversary of the Bishop's death, came at a time of harvest in England.

Switzerland: August 1st is the anniversary of the formation, in 1291, of the oldest continuing government of our civilization.

Syllepsis: In the Greek Orthodox Church, the feast of the Immaculate Conception is called the Syllepsis (Conception) of the Mother of God.

St. Sylvester: The feast day of St. Sylvester was established in the Roman Church as December 31st. *Sylvesterabend* in Austria is celebrated especially as a time for the purification of buildings. But throughout Europe both children and adults join in New Year's Eve merrymaking, the significance of the saint's day being lost in the larger ebullience. In many places, however, the term "St. Sylvester's Eve" still obtains for this occasion. Sylvester I was Pope of the Roman Catholic Church in the fourth century.

Tabernacles: The Jewish Feast of the Tabernacles is celebrated fifteen days after the New Year in the month of Tishri. It is designated by two names, *Asif* or The Ingathering, Succoth or the Feast of Booths. Originally part of a seasonal celebration of the ingathering of summer crops and fruits, the Feast of Tabernacles is therefore part of the period of festivity known as the Feast of Ingathering. There is reason to believe that the harvest season which began the new year included, in a less restrictive sense, nearly all of the month of Tishri. The most significant date of this fall season, the Day of Memorial, is now celebrated as the New Year (also called the Day of Purgation or the Day of Atonement). The seven-day festival of the Ingathering follows. The date varies according to lunar calculations; it may fall between the 10th and 18th of October.

The term "Tabernacles" derives from succoth or booths in which, in early days, families lived during the harvest period. During their Flight from Captivity the Israelites made themselves similarly contrived wattled cabins. The Feast of Tabernacles therefore has historical significance as a commemoration of the escape from bondage in Egypt. The seventh and eighth days of *Succoth* bear the names *Hossanah Rabba* and *Shemini Azareth* (which see).

T'ai Yang: Chinese celebrated the birthday of the King of the Day, the Sun, or T'ai Yang, on the second day of the Second Moon. Yang, the principle of masculine powers, is opposed, in Chinese philosophy and morphology, to that of Yin, the feminine aspect of life.

T'ai Yin: On the fifteenth day of the eighth or "Harvest Moon" Chinese traditionally celebrated the three-day festival of the Birthday of the Moon, or T'ai Yin. This is a day of thanksgiving, of gratitude for crops and life; further, it marks the anniversary of the Festival of Liberation, T'wan Yuan Chieh or Reunion of the Chinese people with their Emperor who was captured during the period of Mongolian occupation.

Taisho: *Taisho Tenno-Sai*, a national holiday in Japan, is celebrated in honor of the death of the Emperor Hirohito's father, Taisho, on the 25th of December.

Tammuz: On the Jewish calendar, one of four minor fast days, this falls on the 17th of Tammuz, the tenth month on the civil calendar. First mentioned by the prophet Zechariah, these fast days were, presumably, instituted at the time of the Babylonian Exile. The 17th of Tammuz (*Shibeah Asar l'Tammuz*) commemorates the first breach made in the walls of the

Temple by Nebuchadnezzar's army and the Roman entrance into the city in 70 C.E.

Tanabata: The Japanese Festival of the Milky Way, analogous to *Chi Hsi,* which see.

Tango-No-Sekku: The Japanese Boys' Festival (May 5th) is characterized by the traditional paper fish—carps several yards long—which are flown in the wind to remind the male heirs of the family that they must be strong as the fish that climbs the waterfall.

Taranaki: The province of Taranaki, New Zealand, celebrates its territorial anniversary on March 31st, or the Monday nearest that date.

Tebet: One of four minor fasts of the Jewish year, the Fast of the Tenth Month falls on the 10th day of Tebet (*Asarah be-Tebet*), the fourth civil and tenth sacred month of the Jewish calendar. This fast commemorates the beginning of Nebuchadnezzar's seige of the Temple at Jerusalem in the year 588.

Tencho Setsu: The birthday of the reigning Emperor of Japan is one of four major holidays of the Japanese year. During the reign of Emperor Hirohito it was celebrated on April 29th.

Teng Chieh: The Chinese Feast of Lanterns or Feast of the Full Moon falls on the 15th day of the First Moon; it is traditionally a New Year celebration analogous to the Japanese Feast of O-Bon.

Tenth Month Fast: See *Tebet.*

Texas Independence: Celebrated on March 2nd on the anniversary of the birth of General Sam Houston, Texas Independence Day commemorates the Battle of San Jacinto at which Santa Anna was defeated and Texas declared an independent republic, free from Mexico's rule (1836-45).

Thanksgiving: An American holiday celebrating the day on which the Pilgrims gave thanks for their first harvest. Edward Winslow, one of the Mayflower travelers, wrote of the occasion that "Our harvest being gotten in, our governor sent four men on fowling, that so we might, after a special manner, rejoice together after we had gathered the fruit of our labours." Governor William Bradford proclaimed this first celebration in 1621 or 1622. In 1795 President Washington "recommended to all . . . to set apart and observe Thursday, the 19th day of February next, as a day of public thanksgiving and prayer," but the occasion was not nationally observed as Thanksgiving Day until after the Civil War. Mrs. Sarah Josepha Hale, of New Hampshire, worked for seventeen years to promote legislation which would make this a national holiday.

Theophany: The Manifestation; see *Epiphany*.

Thiersee's Passion Play: The *Passionspiele* at Thiersee, a village in the Austrian Tyrol, is each year performed by the inhabitants of this locality. The tradition, descendent from much earlier times, amounts to a continued unofficial summer festival of special spiritual significance.

Third Sunday After Epiphany: A day of obligation commemorating Christ's miraculous cure of the leper and the centurion's servant. (Matthew 8:1-13).

Thirty-Third of Omer: See Lag b'Omer.

St. Thomas: The Feast Day of St. Thomas the Apostle (called Didymus) is celebrated by the Greek Orthodox Church on May 13, on December 21st by the Roman Catholic Church, where it was entered on the church calendar in the twelfth century. Thomas, a missionary to the Medes, Persians, Ethiopians and Indians, was martyred at Melapoor, in India. The English custom of dispensing small gifts to those who sought dispensations on this day probably stems from stories relating to St. Thomas's distribution of riches with which, according to legend, he was to have built a great palace for Gondolforus, an Indian emperor. The custom has given this occasion the name of Doeling or Mumping (Begging) Day, terms preferred in some parts of the British Isles.

The feast day of St. Thomas Becket, bishop and martyr, is celebrated December 29th.

The feast day of St. Thomas Aquinas, confessor and Doctor of the Church, is celebrated March 7th. Called the "Angelic Doctor" and the Great Synthesizer, St. Thomas Aquinas is the central figure of scholastic philosophy. He is the patron of schools and the author of many works, including the *Summa Theologica*.

Threading the Needle: See *Chi Hsi*.

Three Archbishops: In the Greek Orthodox Church the three archbishops who are especially remembered for their preservation of ancient Greek culture as well as for their saintly works are remembered together on January 30th. They are Basil the Great, Gregory the Theologian, and John Chrysostom.

Three Kings: See *Epiphany*, or *Twelfth Day*. The Three Kings were Caspar, Melchior and Balthasar.

Thursday: The day sacred to Thor, a Teutonic god apparently much worshiped, for he was friendly to man and an enemy to demons. In some ways Thor might be considered analogous to Zeus of Greek mythology. See also *Great Thursday*.

St. Timothy: One of the missionary companions of the Apostle Paul and several times mentioned in the New Testament, Timothy is primarily known through the latter's pastoral epistles addressed to Timothy, who is presumed to have been bishop at Ephesus and martyred there in 97 A.D. during the reign of Diomitian. His feast day is celebrated in the Latin Church on January 24th, on January 22nd in the Greek Orthodox Church.

Tishri: The first civil month of the Jewish calendar. The 1st of Tishri commemorates the New Year. (See *Blowing of the Trumpets*.) The 3rd of Tishri is celebrated as a minor fast day, also called the Fast of the Seventh Month since Tishri is the seventh sacred month of the calendar, or the Fast of Gedaliah, in commemoration of the slaying of Gedaliah, Governor of Palestine under Nebuchadnezzar.

St. Titus: The birthday of St. Titus, now celebrated on January 4th, marks the last day of the Feast of the Holy Innocents. Titus accompanied St. Paul to Jerusalem (Gal. 2:3); he was later made Bishop of Crete about the year 65.

Tod Kathin: In Thailand an annual occasion for bringing

gifts to the monks. Each young man in Thailand is, for some time, a monk. Royal processions on this occasion (in October) are especially noteworthy.

Tools: See *Visvakarma Puja.*

Touching for the Evil: Magical powers ascribed by rustic people to their kings have frequently been associated with a special day. In England the practice of the king's touching (known merely as the "King's Evil") was specifically appointed by Charles II to fall on January 9th. The practice itself, not the date, is historically verified in English history as far back as the Norman invasion.

Tragic Lovers: See *Chi Hsi.*

Transfer: In the Virgin Islands the anniversary of March 31st, 1917, the day on which the United States took possession of this territory, is marked by local celebrations.

Transfiguration: The Feast of the Transfiguration commemorates Christ's experience upon the mountain, described in Matthew 17.

Thomas Becket: Conflict between Henry II and Thomas á Becket, which led to the latter's murder in 1170, eventually made the martyr a saint in the eyes of the people of his time. Though Becket's shrine was removed at the Reformation, the anniversary of his death remained for centuries as a popular holiday.

Trees: See *New Year for Trees.*

Trenton: Celebration of the anniversary of the Battle of Trenton, New Jersey, has not recently been observed. During the nineteenth century, however, this was a popular occasion on which local groups would re-enact the British defeat December 26, 1776.

Trinity: During the first thousand years of Christian theological history, the dogma of the Holy Trinity, while an accepted part of the creed, was not celebrated at a particular time. During the period of the Arian heresy, however, a Mass was introduced into the Roman Church which later became popular among the Franks. This special Mass was officially entered upon the church calendar by Pope John XXII in 1334.

Observance of Trinity Sunday was introduced into the English Church by St. Thomas Becket in the twelfth century. It is celebrated in May, on the first Sunday after Pentecost.

Trumpets: For Rosh Ha-Shanah or the Feast of the Trumpets, see *Blowing of the Trumpet.*

Tsao Chun: The Chinese Festival of the Kitchen God is of ancient origin. Annual tribute was paid this gaudy and difficult personage on the 23rd day of the Twelfth Moon or, in some provinces, on the 24th day.

Tuan Wu: The Chinese Dragon Boat Festival is one of three annual occasions of settling accounts. It falls on the 5th day of the Fifth Moon. Originally to honor Ch'u Yuan, princely patriot of the Chou Dynasty, the day is observed by dragon-boat racing. For twenty-three hundred years dragon boats have each year raced to a designated place on the river to be the first to offer rice and sweets to the departed spirit of Ch'u Yuan. This day also provides a special occasion for incurring the favor of the dragon spirit, principle of beneficence in nature and of spring and rain.

Tuesday: The day of the week which derives its name from the Teutonic god Tyr (or *Tir* or *Tiwes*) analogous to the Roman Mars.

Tung Chih: Traditional Chinese Feast of the Winter Solstice.

T'Wan Yuan Chieh: See *T'ai Yin,* Chinese Reunion Day.

Twelfth Day: Popular term for Epiphany; also called Old Christmas Day, since it falls on January 6th which was, before the change of styles, the date on which Christmas was celebrated. In early times Epiphany lasted twelve days, the first and last of these being especially important; hence the first came to be called simply Twelfth Day. See *Epiphany* and *Carnival.*

Tyvendedagen: Among the Norwegians Tyvendedagen or Twentieth Day marks the end of the Christmas season and the last (twentieth day) of holiday festivities.

Union of South Africa: In South Africa Union Day, May 31st, marks the forming of the Union of South Africa, in 1906, under the direction of Jan Smuts. The Union of South Africa was created out of the provinces of Cape of Good Hope, Natal, Transvaal, and the Orange Free State.

United Nations: The adoption of the United Nations Charter by fifty nations who originally sent representatives to San Francisco in April, 1945, was declared an anniversary in 1947 at the 101st plenary meeting of the General Assembly and is now observed by most of the member nations.

Unleavened Bread: During the Jewish Passover the initial ceremony known as *pesah* is followed by a six-day festival called the Feast of Unleavened Bread, during which time no work is done, nor fermented food eaten. See *Passover.*

Urs: During May many persons in India make a pilgrimage to Ajmer in celebration of the annual Urs festival. There they worship at the shrine of Khwaja Moin-uddim Chishti, regarded as the prince of Moslem saints in India.

St. Vaclav: *Den Svateho Vaclava* is celebrated September 28th. Especially in Czechoslovakia this is a national holiday in honor of the tenth-century martyr, St. Wenceslas, Duke of Bohemia.

Vainikins: The Feast of Beinging of Wreaths is an ancient Lithuanian festival similar in some respects to May Day. Young people gather branches and adorn themselves with flowers. Under an arbor arch, the young man selects his sweetheart.

Vaisakha Purnima: See *Buddha Vaisakha Purnima;* also *Wesak.*

Valentine: The St. Valentine who most probably became patron of this day was never canonized. It is likely that the celebration goes far back into antiquity, however, for at the Roman Lupercalia it was the custom for young men to draw the names of their partners for the annual dances from a lottery. The modern date of celebration, February 14th, also marks Old Candlemas.

Van Riebeeck: April 6th, anniversary of the landing of the first white settlers in South Africa in 1652.

Vapunpaiva: May Day in Finland is especially celebrated by university students as the opening of the spring season.

Varsa: Buddhist Lent, beginning about July, is celebrated for three months.

Vasana Pravarna: A Buddhist festival in India commemorating the emergence from seclusion of the Buddhist monks. The Bhikkus or monks spend four months in preparation for their eight-month mission in the world. Vasana Pravarna, coming at the end of the rainy season, marks the reactivation of social and religious activities.

Vasant Panchami: The fifth day of Magh, in January or February, is especially sacred to Hindus who honor Saraswati, goddess of learning, also known as Shri Panchami. This day marks the advent of spring in India.

Venezuela: Venezuela was the first country of South America to declare her independence from Spain—July 5, 1811.

Vernal Equinox: The time of the spring at which night and day are equal as the sun crosses the equator from south to north, the day varying from the twentieth to the twenty-third of the month. Whereas both the winter and summer solstices are remarkable for the number and variety of festival rites proceeding from earliest times, observance of the equinoxes is somewhat more common among Eastern peoples; few Western holidays appear to have originated in these events.

Veterans: Formerly Armistice Day, November 11th. The name was changed by act of Congress, June 1, 1954, to honor veterans of both great wars, since Armistice Day had previously been associated exclusively with World War I.

Victoria: The anniversary of the reigning sovereign's birthday is observed throughout the British Empire, but the observance of Queen Victoria's Day—"Empire Day," as it is sometimes called—has special significance for India, Australia, Canada and other Dominions and dependencies.

Victories of Rama: See *Ram Lila*.

Victory: In Colorado, Tennessee, Texas and Hawaii the term "Victory Day" is generally used instead of Armistice Day, or Veterans' Day for November 11th. (Rhode Island celebrates "Victory Day" on the 14th of August.)

Visitation: Celebration of the Virgin Mary's visit to Elizabeth, mother of John the Baptist, is observed July 12th.

Visvakarma Puja: The Festival of Tools is a uniquely Hindu festival celebrated at the end of the sixth month of the Hindu year. At this time Visvakarma, patron of artisans, is worshiped.

Visakha Puja: May. Commemorates the birth, inspiration and death of the Buddha, all three of which events occurred on full moon of May.

St. Vitus: St. Vitus, as far as may be determined, was a boy from Sicily who, converted to Christianity by his nurse, fled from his noble father and suffered martyrdom at a very early age during the reign of Diocletian. His blessing was invoked, among other things, for cure of the disease of chorea, which subsequently came to be known as St. Vitus's Dance.

Walpurgis Night: May Day Eve was, by Teutonic and Nordic tradition, the night on which witches rode to rendezvous on Brocken or some other high mountain. The occasion is popularly celebrated, in some Scandinavian countries, with bonfires and songs.

Washington: George Washington's Birthday was first celebrated in 1781 when Count de Rochambeau acknowledged the friendship of France and the United States by ordering special observance of the birthday of the American Army's Commander-in-Chief. At that time, by the old calendar, the date fell on the 11th of the month, but by 1790 the 22nd was generally adopted as the accepted date. Washington's Birthday has been made a legal holiday in every state in the Union, as well as Alaska, D.C., Hawaii and Puerto Rico.

Water: Sanctified blessing of the waters is a solemn ceremony in many Balkan countries, as far east as the Danube, and in certain European countries, notably Belgium. Officials of the church and state or city proceed to the water's edge in procession, ikons are blessed and washed with salt, etc. Local customs may extend the celebrations generally observed at Epiphany. In Belgium, at the port of Ostend, and in Armenia, Epiphany occurs in July, according to the calendar of the Roman Church. Ceremonies are therefore linked to spring festival celebrations. Among the Hungarians and in port towns of the Danube, Epiphany, by the calendar of the Greek Orthodox Church, falls on January 6th, and similar ceremonies take place on this date. A Greek settlement of sponge fishermen at Tarpon Springs, Florida, celebrate this ceremony on January 6th, which is locally known as Greek Cross Day. See Epiphany.

Weather: Weather prognostication has been so intimately associated with saint days and holidays as to verify their entirely local nature and origin. Rain on St. Medarus' Day in Belgium, for instance, indicates forty more wet days are forthcoming. Rain on St. Swithin's Day in England, on Forty Saints' Day in Rumania or Ground-hog Day in America, have similar associations.

Wednesday: This day derives its name from Wodan (Woden or Wuotan), the greatest of the Teutonic gods, the god of wind and storm.

Weeks: A Jewish festival of thanksgiving for the harvest, referred to in the Bible as the Feast of the Harvest and "the Day of the First Fruits" (Ex. 23:16 and Num. 28:26 respectively). Because the grain harvest lasted seven weeks in Palestine, it also was called the Feast of Weeks, celebrated fifty days after Passover. From this circumstance was derived the term "Pentecost," Greek word for "fifty." Because the giving of the Ten Commandments nearly coincided with the Feast of Weeks, the festival came to be considered the spiritual birthday of Israel, the anniversary of God's Covenant with His people. Pentecost symbolizes the reaffirmation of that bond; the holiday falls on the 6th day of Sivan, third sacred month of the Jewish lunar calendar. (See *Shabuoth.*)

The early Christian Church adopted the Jewish usage with this difference, that the entire season from Easter to Whitsunday (specifically corresponding to Pentecost) is known as "Pentecost," a festive period during which no fasts were kept and the church grew festive in honor of Christ's resurrection.

Wellington: The province of Wellington, New Zealand, celebrates its territorial anniversary in public observances on January 22nd, or the Monday nearest that date.

Wesak: The day on which Buddha was born, celebrated (usually) in May among followers of the great Lord. "Wesak" is the Singhalese name for one of the days of the full moon.

In some Buddhist countries, such as Thailand, Wesak festivals (there called Wisakha Buja) commemorate the birth, enlightenment and passing into Nirvana of the Lord Buddha and continue for a number of days. In Japan Wesak Day is celebrated the first Sunday of the month of April.

West Virginia: In commemoration of the admission of West Virginia into the Union in 1863, West Virginia Day is observed on June 20th as a legal holiday in that state.

Westland: The province of Westland, New Zealand, celebrates its territorial anniversary in public observances on December 1st or the Monday nearest.

White Week: In Albania the week preceding Lent is called Jav'e Bardhe, or "The White Week," and during this time no meat is eaten, only dairy products.

Whitsunday: The English word "Whitsunday" (White Sunday) originated in the custom of newly baptized persons presenting themselves for service all dressed in white. Whitsunday derives its meaning and associations from the Jewish feast of Pentecost. Originally it lasted seven days but was limited, in 1094, to three days; Tuesday was abolished in 1711, and, by order of Pope Pius X in 1911, Monday was excepted as a day of holy obligation. Nevertheless, most European countries still observe the Monday following Whitsunday as a legal holiday. Whitsunday marks the first day of the fourth and last Ember week marking the *hiemale* or winter season of the year. See *Pentecost* and *Weeks*.

Wildlife Restoration Week: Sponsored by the National Wildlife Federation, Washington, D.C., the third week in April is designated and especially remembered by several thousand clubs throughout America.

Will Carleton: See *Carleton*.

Will Rogers: See *Rogers*.

Willow Sunday: In the Eastern (Russian) Orthodox Church, and notably in Bulgaria, Czechoslovakia and the Ukraine, the Sunday before Easter is known as Willow Sunday. Branches of pussy willows gathered on Lazarus Saturday are carried to the church and blessed. These may later be placed in the home as omens of good fortune.

Wilson: Woodrow Wilson's Birthday, December 28th. In 1928 South Carolina made this date a state holiday.

World War II: Arkansas celebrates August 14th as World War II Day in preference to Veterans' Day, November 11th.

St. Wulfstan: As Saxon Bishop of Worcester at the time of the Norman Conquest, Wulfstan was brought before Norman bishops and barons. He was told that his ignorance of the French language must keep him from exercising his duties. The Bishop thereupon struck with his staff of office upon the tomb of Edward the Confessor, and the staff imbedded itself so deeply in the stone that the Normans reconsidered their judgment. The last saint of the Anglo-Saxon Church, St. Wulfstan is remembered on January 19th.

Yama: The Hindu holiday especially devoted to brothers and sisters. On the 5th day of Diwali, or Festival of the Garland of Lights, a brother is expected to spend time with his sister and bring her the finest present he can afford. See *Diwali.*

Yaum Al-Jum'ah: See *Adam's Birthday.*

Yom Kippur: The last of ten penitential days beginning with the Blowing of the Trumpet, the first day of the Jewish New Year. It is described (Lev. 16) as set apart by Moses and is one of the principal Jewish holidays, observed both as a day of repentance and as a time for remembering the souls of the dead. Yom Kippur falls on the 10th day of Tishri, the first civil month of the Jewish New Year and falls between October 5th and 13th on the Gregorian calendar. On this day, according to Jewish theological tradition, God closes his books for the year and begins a new ledger of life.

Yom Tob: Jewish days which are in the strictest sense holy days are called Yom Tob.

Yorktown: Anniversary of Lord Cornwallis' surrender at Yorktown, Va., October 19, 1781, has been celebrated at various times in our history. Originally local celebrations of the Revolutionary period involved what was called a "Cornwallis," a sort of masquerade involving a sham fight between British and American troops.

Yuan Tan: The Chinese New Year's Day is also the anniversary of the Chinese Republic and the Revolution of 1912 which precipitated it. Further, it was on this day that Dr. Sun Yat-sen, first President of the Republic, was inaugurated. Traditional observance of new year's day occurred between January 21 and February 19 on the Gregorian calendar, but modern patriotic celebrations are held on January 1st.

Yu Shui: The Chinese festival of Yu Shui, or spring showers, celebrates (in February) the first spring rains and reawakening of life somewhat after the manner of the Buddhist Festival, Vasana Pravarna.

Zarathustra: The religion of the Iranian (Aryan) people was founded by Zarathustra, meaning "out of Persia" (Greek corruption, "Zoroaster"). It is mentioned by Xanthus and Plato, but the date of origin is not known; it flourished from about the sixth century B.C. until the Mohammedan invasion of India in 636. At the present time the Parsee are the greatest aggregation of followers of Zarathustra. The anniversary of his birth, called the Khordadsal, is celebrated on the 6th day of the first Parsee month, Farvardin.

Zrinski-Frankopan: A Croatian national day (April 30th), anniversary of the deaths of Count Peter Zrinski and the Marquis Francis of Frankopan, who attempted to unite the Croatian people and to secure their country's independence from Austria in the seventeenth century.